brilliant

relationships

relationships

Your ultimate guide to attracting and keeping the perfect partner

2nd edition

Annie Lionnet

PEARSON

Harlow, England • London • New York • Boston • San Francisco • Toronto • Sydney • Auckland • Singapore • Hong Kong
Tokyo • Seoul • Taipei • New Delhi • Cape Town • São Paulo • Mexico City • Madrid • Amsterdam • Munich • Paris • Milan

PEARSON EDUCATION LIMITED

Edinburgh Gate
Harlow CM20 2JE
Tel: +44 (0)1279 623623
Fax: +44 (0)1279 431059
Website: www.pearsoned.com/uk

First published in Great Britain in 2008
Second edition published 2012

© Pearson Education Limited 2008, 2012

Pearson Education is not responsible for the content of third-party internet sites.

ISBN: 978-0-273-77040-4

British Library Cataloguing-in-Publication Data
A catalogue record for this book is available from the British Library

Library of Congress Cataloging-in-Publication Data
Lionnet, Annie.
  Brilliant relationships : your ultimate guide to attracting and keeping the
  perfect partner / Annie Lionnet.-- 2nd ed.
     p. cm.
  ISBN 978-0-273-77040-4 (pbk.)
  1. Man-woman relationships. I. Title.
  HQ801.L487 2012
  306.7--dc23
                        2011049070

10 9 8 7 6 5 4 3 2 1
15 14 13 12 11

Typeset in 10/14pt Plantin by 30
Printed and bound in Great Britain by Henry Ling Ltd., at the Dorset Press,
Dorchester, Dorset

Contents

'Love has no desire but to fulfil itself. But if you love and must needs have desires, let these be your desires: To melt and be like a running brook that sings its melody to the night. To know the pain of too much tenderness. To be wounded by your own understanding of love; and to bleed willingly and joyfully. To wake at dawn with a winged heart and give thanks for another day of loving; to rest at the noon hour and meditate love's ecstasy; to return home at eventide with gratitude; and then to sleep with a prayer for the beloved in your heart and a song of praise upon your lips.'

Kahlil Gibran, mystical writer and poet

'For one human being to love another: that is perhaps the most difficult task of all ... the work for which all other work is but preparation. It is a high inducement to the individual to ripen ... a great exacting claim upon us, something that chooses us out and calls us to vast things.'

Rainer Maria Rilke, poet and novelist

About the author

Annie Lionnet is a life transformation coach with many years' experience in the field of personal development. She brings her love of life and people, of science and spirituality to her unique coaching service, working with both individual clients and groups. With her trademark warmth, she inspires and guides her clients to create – and live – their best lives. Her mission is to help others find the keys to self-empowerment within themselves, and thus live a life of joyful authenticity. Annie is also a professional astrologer and combines astrology with coaching to give you a sense of your own uniqueness and how to live that in the world. She is the director of Affordable Life Coaching (www.affordablelifecoaching.org), an organisation that believes in the innate potential of people to live meaningful and fulfilled lives. As well as publishing books on coaching and personal development, Annie has written books on astrology and the tarot. You can read more about her at: www.annielionnet.co.uk.

Acknowledgements

I would like to thank everyone who has come into my life to help shape my experience and understanding of love and relationships. You know who you are and I am deeply grateful to you all.

Foreword

Love is a force of destiny whose power reaches from heaven to hell.

Carl Jung, psychiatrist

How much time and energy do you spend thinking about relationships? Are you happy with the status quo right now or do you long for more passion, intimacy and connection with your partner? And if you are single, how are you feeling about your chances of meeting your perfect match? We have an inbuilt desire to relate to another person, which underpins our drive to form relationships. For some of us this desire is easily expressed, while others find it harder truly to connect with another human being. There is something immensely courageous in us that lets us risk opening our hearts to another. A safe passage is never guaranteed in love, and none of us know where the journey will take us, how long it will last or what we will experience along the way. What we do know is that we feel more alive, expanded and whole when we feel love – both for ourselves and for our partners.

Love is a fundamental need that we all share. Without love we cannot feel truly happy and fulfilled. No matter how successful, accomplished or self-aware we are, true joy comes from sharing who we are with another, whether it be in an intimate relationship or some other kind of loving relationship. But we can feel deeply ambivalent about this and we aren't always open to revealing ourselves in a relationship. For many of us, becoming intimate and exposing our true selves can be both a wish and a dread. So how do we overcome our fears and learn to open our hearts and experience a deep and loving connection in our relationships? What is required of us? If you are willing to grow, and you are ready to invite more love into your life and enjoy a deeply fulfilling and intimate relationship, then this book is for you. Enjoy the journey.

Introduction

The meeting of two personalities is like the contact of two chemical substances. If there is a reaction, both are transformed.

Carl Jung, psychiatrist

Are you in the kind of relationship that you've always dreamt of? Or does the state of play between you and your partner leave much to be desired? And if you're not in a relationship, are you longing for the right person to come into your life but don't seem to attract them?

Everyone dreams of finding the perfect mate. We have all been brought up on fairy tales that tell us that we will live happily ever after, once we find that other person – our other half. The term itself suggests we are incomplete until we find that special someone. In fact our very well-being would seem to depend on how successful our relationships are.

Relationships – at least the good ones – enrich and enhance our lives and make us feel more alive. They are precious gifts which enable us to grow, discover more about who we are and expand into a fuller, more joyful sense of ourselves. Relationships also challenge us to look at ourselves, recognise and accept the parts of our personality that we don't like or are unaware of, and understand why we behave in certain ways.

Virtually everyone has the potential to create a brilliant relationship, no matter where you are in your life or what your personal history is. But in order to do this, you need to be willing to let go of your preconceived ideas and spend some time getting to know what's right for you and what makes you happy. Then you can start to focus on attracting your perfect match or bringing more sparkle into your existing relationship.

So, how do we achieve the quality of relationship we are seeking? And is this within our control? We do have a choice. We can either struggle to preserve the outdated fantasies and old models of relationships, even though they don't match reality or offer any real hope of happiness. Or we can learn to see the challenges we are currently experiencing in finding our perfect match or feeling fulfilled in our partnerships as opportunities to create a completely new concept of relationships.

> relationships can be a way of reaching a deeper understanding of what makes us and our partners tick

If we choose the latter approach, relationships can be a way of reaching a deeper understanding of what makes us and our partners tick. That awareness enables us to be clear about what we want and how to fulfil our needs. Without that understanding we are groping in the dark. So if you're not in a relationship, how do you find love? And if you are in a relationship, how do you keep it alive and growing?

There isn't one single answer to these questions. But as you read this book think of it more like a process in which you gradually discover how to have the best relationship with yourself and your partner, or, if you are single, how to attract the right partner for you. Each chapter takes you deeper into the process and is designed to give you guidance, insight and inspiration on how to:

- increase your self-worth and what you feel you deserve;
- recognise the value of being alone and embrace having time to yourself;
- break recurring negative patterns;
- let go of the past and move on;
- make more conscious choices when selecting a partner;
- attract your perfect match;
- master the art of keeping your relationship healthy and happy.

When we are in a fulfilling relationship, the world seems a more colourful, expansive and bountiful place. Conversely, when we long for a relationship or feel unhappy with the one we are in, we can feel deeply lonely and dissatisfied. That doesn't mean that you can't lead a joyful and fulfilled life without a partner. Of course you can. In fact there are times when it's important that you do. Often we need to spend time alone in order to take stock of our lives, heal and develop ourselves in our own right. This, as we will see in Chapters 1 and 4, is an immensely valuable and often essential commitment that we need to make to ourselves if we want to be in an intimate, balanced, respectful and loving relationship. But if we're really honest with ourselves, most of us will admit that no matter how capable we are of being on our own or how hurt we may have been in the past, being in a joyful, supportive and fulfilling relationship is what we truly desire. We want a relationship in which we can thrive and grow and, most importantly, be loved for who we are.

Take stock of your life

So first you need to be willing to take a look at yourself, your relationships both past and present and the choices that you have made to date. This can be challenging – and immensely rewarding – as well as essential if you truly desire to create a brilliant relationship. The key to a happy relationship is choosing the right person. And you can't do that until you know yourself well enough to trust your choices and discover what – and who – you really want. The more aware you become, the more control you have over your choices. In fact understanding why you make the choices you do can make or break a relationship.

 **brilliant** tip

The key to a happy relationship is knowing what you want and how to choose the right person.

The power of relationships

Through our understanding of psychology over the last century it has become apparent that relationships have the potential to:

- fulfil our desires and deepest longings;
- open our hearts;
- connect us with our vulnerability;
- bring out the best – and sometimes the worst – in us;
- expose our 'shadow';
- provide a source of comfort and security;
- alleviate our sense of isolation;
- benefit our health and well-being;
- help us grow and develop;
- offer us greater awareness and a deeper understanding of ourselves, our expectations and the way in which we relate to others.

It is no wonder that we place so much importance on relationships and that they have such a powerful influence in our lives! So where do you start?

One step at a time

The beginning of your journey towards creating a brilliant relationship starts with Chapter 1. This chapter offers you specific insights and tools to help you gain a deeper understanding of yourself and grow in self-awareness. This involves taking the time to get to know yourself better, feeling good about who you are, and committing to a happier and healthier relationship with yourself. Inspirational exercises and questions help you to:

- identify your core values and the importance of honouring them;
- discover your deepest needs and how to fulfil them.

Chapter 2 helps you to take an honest look at your expectations and beliefs. These hold a key to the quality of your relationships and will powerfully influence your choices and experiences. Fortunately, your beliefs and expectations are not written in stone. This chapter shows you how you can transform the ones that limit you and enhance the quality of your relationships.

> good communication is fundamental to a successful relationship

Good communication is fundamental to a successful relationship. In fact how well you and your partner communicate can make or break your relationship. Chapter 3 outlines the successful principles of communication that will help you to resolve conflicts and radically improve the way in which you communicate and interact in relationships.

Chapter 4 focuses on breaking up and moving on and will help you to recognise when a relationship is over, navigate the pitfalls of this difficult transition, understand the importance of letting go and feel positive about creating a new life. Then Chapter 5 on the space in between shows you all the different ways in which you can come into your own when you are not in an intimate relationship and feel really good about this stage in your life.

Most of us have found ourselves repeating patterns in our relationships. Even when we think we have moved on, we can suddenly find ourselves in an all too familiar scenario without understanding how we got ourselves there. Chapter 6 demystifies this phenomenon and offers clear guidance on how to recognise and change negative patterns and create much more fulfilling relationships.

Chapter 7 gives you specific insights into how to become more confident and attract your perfect match – in other words, the one that works best for you. Discover the secrets of the law of attraction and what makes you irresistible.

Chapter 8 stresses the importance of creating an equal relationship in which both you and your partner feel authentic and empowered. You'll discover how to transform power struggles into more equal relationships and balance your own needs with those of your partner.

Letting go of the past can be one of our greatest challenges. So often we hang on to unresolved emotions such as grief or anger from a previous relationship and this blocks our chances of happiness in the present. Chapter 9 gives clear examples and guidance on how to heal past wounds and free yourself from your past once and for all.

When you lovingly tend a garden everything in it thrives. Think of your relationship in the same way. Chapter 10 shows you how to cultivate your relationship so that it flourishes. Find out how to keep a relationship from going to seed, and discover ways in which to keep growing and discovering new things about yourself and your partner. This chapter gives you the tools to enjoy greater intimacy and deeper fulfilment with your partner. Falling in love and being in an intimate relationship can make us feel very vulnerable and as a result we can become quite fearful. Find out how to let go of control, and learn to trust and engage wholeheartedly in your relationship.

Living happily ever after doesn't mean that you will never again experience a difficult patch in your relationships. So you need to be confident in your ability to resolve any problems that arise. In the last chapter the ten essential principles of a successful relationship are revealed.

Whether you're single or attached, ready to meet someone or wary of getting involved again, the journey on which you are about to embark will inspire you to:

● have the best relationship with both yourself – a prerequisite for having a great relationship – and your partner;

● become a magnet for your perfect match.

So, are you ready to take the plunge and commit to discovering more about you, and become an expert at creating and enjoying a deeply fulfilling intimate relationship? If the answer is yes, then turn the page and take the next step.

CHAPTER 1

Get to know you

The best thing we can do for our relationships with others is to render our relationship with ourselves more conscious.

James Hollis, Jungian analyst

We are all familiar with the Ancient Greek aphorism, 'know yourself'. But what does it really mean? And how much importance do you put on this deceptively simple imperative? It may come as a surprise to discover that the quality of your relationships depends on the quality of your relationship with yourself. The truth is that we cannot be happy, honest, authentic and intimate with our partner unless we are able to be those things with ourselves. This involves establishing our own identity and having a clear sense of our feelings and preferences and what we desire. If we don't know these things about ourselves, how can we hope to share them with a partner, or indeed anyone else?

We need to know how we feel and what's important to us if we are to create successful relationships. We also need to know and accept the different parts of ourselves and recognise that when we feel comfortable with ourselves, we are much more attractive and magnetic to others. We literally draw them to us.

 **brilliant** action

To help you on your way to understanding yourself and your relationship patterns better, take a moment to consider the following questions. Be completely honest with yourself, as this is the first requirement for any successful relationship.

● Can you be completely yourself and still be loved?
● Can you be loving and yet not be responsible for your partner's well-being?
● Do you seek constant assurances that your partner loves you?
● Have you ever stayed in a relationship even though you weren't really happy?
● Have you ever taken a partner back because you felt you couldn't live without them/were afraid of being alone?
● Do you hold on to past resentments from old relationships?
● Do you think it's possible to take care of your own needs and not be selfish? If so, how?

Spend a few minutes thinking about your answers. Do some of them raise more questions? Is there anything that you would like to change? If so, where do you start?

brilliant tip

When we know and accept who we are, we are much more attractive and magnetic to others.

Feel good about you

Before you begin to look at your relationships, you need to focus on your relationship with yourself. It's an old cliché, but you can't hope to love or be loved by another wholeheartedly if you don't have a positive regard for yourself. So if your self-esteem – or lack of it – is undermining your ability to be happy in a relationship, now is the time to begin improving it. Feeling good about who and what you are develops over time, so the sooner you start the better.

Self-love

Through thick and thin on life's journey the one person who is always living each experience with you is you. Even if you have a committed and supportive relationship, only you can ever be 100 per cent present in your life. So it's essential that you like being you and enjoy your own company. Understanding that we cannot love another without first loving ourselves is the key to any healthy relationship. This concept of self-love is based on the premise that we need to love and accept ourselves unconditionally – our strengths and our weaknesses. In practice, this means recognising our shortcomings and negative traits without judgement. That doesn't

> we cannot love another without first loving ourselves

mean that we resign ourselves to those aspects of our nature that undermine and diminish us. It simply means that when we start from a place of acceptance, we are no longer in conflict with ourselves. This frees up our energy and enables us to focus on ways to become happier and more fulfilled.

All of us possess positive and negative characteristics. Self-love is about having a positive regard for ourselves, no matter what physical, intellectual or emotional attributes we have. Whether you see yourself as gorgeous or unattractive, intelligent or average, confident or shy, begin to see yourself in a positive light. Your strengths, weaknesses, talents and imperfections are all part of what makes you unique. As you acquire a conscious acceptance of all of who you are, both positive and negative, you will begin to transform the quality of your life and your relationships.

Self-love is about:

- learning to be your own best friend;
- accepting that you are human and therefore flawed;
- committing to growth and becoming the best possible you;
- being willing to challenge yourself;
- becoming whole by embracing all of who you are.

 **action**

Think about all the things that you like about yourself and write them down. This can be challenging, because we often have an inbuilt resistance to focusing on ourselves in this way and we tend to play down our attributes. Nevertheless, before you decide what it is that you would love and value in a partner, you need to know who you are and acknowledge what makes *you* special.

What I like about myself is:

1

2

3

4

5

6

7

8

9

10

How easy was it for you to do this exercise? Did you notice any reluctance or resistance to affirming yourself? Loving and appreciating yourself is the foundation to a fulfilling relationship, so have another look at your list and, if you're feeling bold, say each one out loud. You might try looking in the mirror as you affirm all of these positive things about yourself. Keep adding to your list. If you run out of things that you like about yourself, think about all the compliments that you've been given and see whether you can 'own' the qualities that others see in you. More often than not, we 'project' our positive qualities on to those we admire, not realising that they belong to us.

Unmask your true self

As children we learn to hide our real feelings and mask our real selves in an attempt to fit in, be accepted by others and protect ourselves from possible hurt. We adopt a persona – a false self – which belies the truth of who we really are. Our persona often gives others the impression that we are more confident and independent than we really are. While this can facilitate our contact with others, when we identify too strongly with our persona we risk becoming alienated from our true nature. When this happens we lack authenticity and feel out of synch with ourselves and the rest of the world. We aren't able to express our true thoughts and feelings and others don't see us for who we really are.

When we create a false impression of ourselves we don't know what we really want and need. And we can't possibly hope to create an honest relationship because we are, in effect, deceiving both ourselves and others. The Danish philosopher Kierkegaard noted that the most common form of despair is that of not being who we really are, adding that an even deeper form of despair comes from choosing to be someone other than oneself.

So how can we connect with our true self? In order to move beyond our persona and expose our real self, the first thing we need to do is be willing to take a risk.

The power of self-awareness

If you want a relationship in which you are accepted for your true self, you need to be honest with yourself about who you are. This can feel risky, because we are often afraid of what we might find in the process of self-discovery. Bringing the different parts of us to light can be challenging, but the more we can integrate these facets, the more balanced and whole we feel. Carl Jung, the Swiss psychoanalyst, used the word 'individuation' to describe the conscious realisation of our uniqueness, including both strengths and limitations. As we become more self-aware – or individuate – our personalities unfold and we discover our true identity. When we no longer need to pretend to be something we're not, we feel authentic and alive, and we have the confidence to be who we naturally are. The paradox of individuation is that by focusing on our own development and becoming more self-aware, we create the context for a rich and rewarding relationship.

> when we no longer need to pretend to be something we're not, we feel authentic and alive

Discover your values

One of the best ways to find out more about yourself is through identifying your values. Your values shape the way you see yourself and the world. They underpin your character and offer you valuable insights into what is really important to you. Knowing what your values are and aligning yourself with them is essential for your well-being and integrity. When you honour your values you are honouring what is intrinsic to you, and this gives a clear message about how you want to be treated by others.

We rarely take the time to consider our values and how they define us. When we lack this awareness it's hard for us to be clear about what we want and need. So how do you know what your values are? Well, when you feel strongly or passionately about something, this will inevitably reflect one of your values. For example, if independence is one of your values, you will rank this very highly and you may experience anger or resentment if it feels threatened. If you value loyalty highly then you are likely to feel very aggrieved if someone behaves disloyally. Discovering and clarifying your values will strengthen and support your sense of self and the choices that you make. When you don't honour your values, you aren't able to stand for who you are. Conversely, when you honour your values, you are being true to yourself and this gives you a sense of internal rightness.

Here is a list of words that illustrate values:

adventure	fun	personal space
assertiveness	generosity	punctuality
autonomy	growth	reflection
beauty	hard working	reliability
collaboration	harmony	romance
communion	honesty	security
connection	humour	success
courage	independence	tenacity
decisiveness	intimacy	tolerance
dependability	joy	trust
excitement	loyalty	truthfulness
fidelity	orderliness	
freedom	partnership	

The easiest way to determine your values is to look at your own life. For example, if you relish the times when you are on your own and see these as a chance to check in with yourself and restore your batteries, two of your values are likely to be personal space and reflection. If you love sharing your innermost being with your loved one, your values are likely to be intimacy, communion and connection. Of course it's possible to have all these values, in which case it's essential to your well-being that each of them is honoured.

 action

Think about your values and list them below. If you can think of more than ten, add them to the list.

My values are:

1

2

3

4

5

6

7

8

9

10

Ask the right questions

Ask yourself what is important about each value. Does your life feel congruent with each of your values? Which ones do you feel you are most in tune with? Do you struggle to honour any of them? Are some more important to you than others? If so, these will be your core values and reflect what is sacred to you. Be careful not to judge yourself as you ask yourself these questions. You are simply checking out what really matters to you and whether your life and your relationships reflect this. Over the coming days and weeks, see if any more of your values emerge and add them to your list. Experiment with different ways in which you can express your values. Notice how you feel when you align yourself with one of your values and how others respond to you. Keep practising being congruent with your values and write down any shifts that take place.

Dare to honour your values

Honouring our values can be challenging if we are afraid of the consequences. For example, one of your values might be honesty, but if you are afraid of what might happen if you speak your mind, you might hold back from speaking your truth. If excitement and adventure are your values and you also value security, you might favour the latter if you fear that your desire for something new might jeopardise your relationship. Ideally, all our values need to be acknowledged and integrated if we are to feel whole and authentic. So even if some of your values appear to be mutually exclusive, be creative and think about ways in which you can be true to them all.

Move out of your comfort zone

Whether we do it consciously or not, we often avoid exploring and cultivating our inner lives and ignore or suppress our feelings. One of the reasons for this is that we are often resistant to change and more interested in the status quo. This becomes our comfort zone, even if we are not feeling good about ourselves and our relationships. Why is that? Often we are reluctant to experience a negative or uncomfortable feeling as we fear that it might overwhelm us or compel us to re-evaluate our lives. For example, we might cling to our romantic illusions and prefer to fantasise about the person of our dreams rather than taking any real responsibility for creating a relationship that will emotionally fulfil us.

Even if that strategy of avoidance and self-protection works for a while, life has a way of forcing our hand, and sooner or later we are required – or compelled – to deal with what is making us unhappy. Often it takes a crisis for us finally to acknowledge how we're really feeling. This is often described as a 'wake-up call', and it can be a very painful experience. However, drastic measures are only required when you've abdicated all responsibility for your own happiness. So is there another way to acquire greater self-awareness and begin to feel more in control of your own happiness? Indeed there is!

Spend quality time with yourself

If you think it's selfish or too time-consuming to focus on you, think again. The expression 'self-centred' has negative connotations, but it simply means that you operate from your own centre of gravity. This gives you a core stability and a strong framework for your life, enabling you to have a more conscious relationship with the most important person in your life – you. When you have this, everyone benefits and you have much more to give to your relationship.

To live a balanced life, we need to be good at both 'doing' and 'being'. We're usually much better at 'doing' – focusing on what we want to achieve and getting caught up in our hurried and busy lives. 'Being', on the other hand, allows us to slow down, become present and connect with how we are feeling. 'Being' allows us to spend time with ourselves and gives us the space to connect more deeply with our true nature, develop our intuition and what it is that is right for us. We often need to make a conscious effort to take time out of our busy lives, slow down and focus on how and where we are. Engaging in 'being' time enables you really to connect with yourself and what needs your attention. It brings you back to yourself and what's really important. When

> to live a balanced life, we need to be good at both 'doing' and 'being'

you focus on 'being' rather than 'doing', you cultivate a loving relationship with yourself and nurture, honour and support your true essence. As you begin to discover and respond to your own needs, you build the foundation for a loving, nurturing and supportive relationship with your partner.

brilliant tip

When we can trust that we will give ourselves what we need, we can trust others to do the same.

Give yourself more pleasure

Make the space for some 'being' time at least a couple of times a day. And remember that 'being' time needs to feel pleasurable. You can start with first thing in the morning and last thing at night, and gradually build in other times during your day. Gradually, this becomes a habit, a positive daily practice, which increasingly strengthens, uplifts and affirms you. When we can trust that we will give ourselves what we need, we can trust others to do the same. Savour your 'being' time as a way of slowing down, being in the moment and giving yourself more pleasure.

brilliant action

The following suggestions will help you to cultivate your 'being' time.

- Take some time every day to do what you love and makes you feel good. Go for a walk in nature. Read. Meditate. Write a journal. Listen to music. Take a warm, fragrant, candlelit bath. Be creative. Be playful. Or just simply relax. Become intimate with yourself.

- Enjoy your own company. Remember you are the one travelling companion that is with you throughout your life.

- Don't be a flat-earther by believing that there is a limit to how far you can explore the parameters of your world. Be adventurous.
- Find a great teacher/mentor/therapist/coach and discover more about yourself.
- Spend time with someone who inspires and energises you.

brilliant tip

When you focus on 'being' rather than 'doing', you nurture, honour and support yourself. This lays the foundation for a loving, nurturing and supportive relationship with your partner.

Take your time

It takes time to know ourselves, our different characteristics and personality traits. We need a mixture of curiosity, courage and commitment to get to know and fully acknowledge all of who we are. And we need to be willing to be in for the long haul. This may seem daunting at first, since we live in a quick-fix society and we often avoid taking the time to cultivate a relationship with ourselves. Perversely, we are often more interested in getting to know others than ourselves. Consider what happens when we fall in love. We want to know everything about that person and we delight in the gradual process of discovering more about them – their thoughts, feelings, passions and aspirations – even their imperfections. Everything about them holds endless fascination. What would happen if you began to see yourself as endlessly fascinating and took the time

> we are often more interested in getting to know others than ourselves

to uncover everything that makes you unique? The likelihood is that you will feel enriched and nurtured and start to savour this delicious relationship with yourself.

Become a whole person

It's vital that we recognise, accept and integrate our various facets, as this gives us a sense of wholeness. When we feel whole we no longer expect a relationship to complete us. We are already complete! This dramatically affects how we feel about ourselves and, in turn, helps us attract the right relationship. The more in touch we are about what we think and feel, the more empowered we are to create a life – and a relationship – that reflects who we are. Becoming more self-aware and whole is a process that ultimately leads you to a much stronger and fuller sense of yourself. When that happens, you acquire a confidence in yourself and a knowing that no matter what the challenges, you feel equal to the task. When you feel whole you are no longer looking for another to fill the void. You have no fear of being in your own right, even if this means risking confrontation or being alone. You know yourself and you take complete responsibility for your happiness. And you feel capable of handling the inevitable ups and downs that occur in life and in relationships. Being a whole person enables you to live a balanced life in which you value both 'being' time and 'doing' time – spending time alone and sharing your life with your partner.

brilliant tip

You prepare the ground for a brilliant relationship when you:

- accept yourself, warts and all;
- recognise that others are also imperfect;
- embrace change and learning.

 **brilliant** example

Cultivating a relationship with yourself

When I met Tania she was feeling empty and confused. Her relationship of 10 years had recently ended and her demanding job was unrewarding. It became apparent that Tania had spent her whole adult life in 'doing' mode and she had never stopped to think about how she really felt or what was important to her. She admitted that she had secretly been afraid to take stock of her life, for fear that it would fall apart. As Tania began to examine her life, she realised that she hadn't been true to herself and that this had led to an unsatisfactory career and an unhappy relationship. Tania discovered that two of her core values were peace and creativity, so I suggested she started writing a journal first thing in the morning and last thing at night. She began to relish these times to herself as opportunities to check in with how she was feeling and put her experiences into words. To her amazement, she discovered that she had a talent for writing and she enrolled on a creative writing course. Giving herself time and space for her own process meant that Tania blossomed and found her own voice.

A work in progress

Think of yourself as a work in progress as you journey towards greater self-awareness and wholeness. As you progress, you will acquire many new perspectives and insights into what is unique about you and what makes you happy. In essence, becoming whole enables you to have a conscious relationship with yourself – the parts you like and the parts that you dislike. Being whole requires giving time to your emotional, mental and physical well-being. When you feel whole you are full of yourself – not in a negative sense, but full of your own emotions, experience, wisdom, ideas and values.

 **brilliant** tip

When we feel whole we no longer expect a relationship to complete us.

 **brilliant** recap

To create a brilliant relationship you first need to spend time getting to know and appreciate yourself. This requires taking time out of your busy life and giving yourself the space to tune in to your needs and what you are feeling. This will give you a strong foundation on which to build a stronger, happier and more self-aware you. From there, you will be in a strong position to attract and maintain a loving and fulfilling relationship.

brilliant task for the week

Consciously give yourself more time for you. Start with 10 minutes a day and notice how this begins to change the way you feel about yourself.

CHAPTER 2

Create positive beliefs and transform your expectations

Whatever we expect with confidence becomes our own self-fulfilling prophecy.

Brian Tracy, self-help author

Whether we are aware of it or not, we all carry certain expectations about relationships. For example, some of us expect to be loved and accepted, while others expect to be let down or criticised. Whatever we have grown to expect, deep down we all want to go through life knowing that we will be supported, encouraged and – most importantly – loved and accepted. And although we are entirely responsible for our own happiness and well-being, it's natural to expect our relationships with others to make a major contribution to our happiness.

While no relationship is perfect, it is perfectly reasonable to expect the following qualities in a relationship:

- honesty, integrity and trust;
- acceptance, tolerance and patience;
- appreciation, encouragement and acknowledgement;
- kindness and affection;
- a willingness to bridge any differences;
- commitment;
- flexibility and freedom;
- forgiveness.

Where do our expectations come from?

We all have an essential need to give and receive love. As babies, we need food and warmth to survive. But unless we are loved, we fail to thrive. If we have been wounded as a result of our need to be loved, we unconsciously create defences to protect ourselves. For example, if a parent withholds love and affection from a child on a repeated basis, that child will learn to stop asking or expecting to be loved. Or if that parent only gives praise or shows affection when the child is obedient or does well, the child will equate love with approval and not expect to be loved simply for who they are.

Unless we become conscious of these early patterns they will carry on operating in our adult relationships. Our expectations play a very significant role in the kind of partners that we attract and are attracted to, and how committed and fulfilling our relationships are. Many of our expectations will be based on our beliefs and experiences to date. Positive, affirming beliefs about ourselves create positive expectations. This also works in reverse. Negative beliefs about ourselves create negative expectations. So what are your beliefs and expectations and what impact do they have on your life?

 **action**

Some of the questions below might feel challenging, especially if it's the first time that you've considered them. When you've given each question some thought, write your answers down. This will help you to know what to focus on.

● What are my beliefs and expectations about attracting my ideal partner?

● What are my beliefs and expectations about being in a relationship?

● What patterns in my relationships do I want to expand/change/no longer create?

- How have my beliefs and expectations impacted on my relationships?
- How have my beliefs and expectations prevented me from creating a fulfilling relationship?
- Do I look to my partner to provide some need or want that I could provide for myself?

Did any of your answers surprise you? Perhaps you are becoming aware for the first time of some of your beliefs and expectations. Do you think any of them might be holding you back or limiting your choices and experiences? Now think about any pay-off that there might be to holding on to a negative belief or a low expectation. This may seem perverse, but when we sabotage our own happiness it's because deep inside we don't feel we deserve to be happy, loved and appreciated. And so we make choices and behave in ways that block our chances of happiness.

Self-talk

Every day we have thousands of internal conversations with ourselves. Self-talk is the most important conversation we will ever have because it shapes the way we see ourselves and the world. When we feel confident, our self-talk is positive and affirming. And we expect the best. But very often we are at the mercy of our more negative internal dialogue and act as if we have no power to control – or change – our thinking. Becoming aware of your self-talk and recognising how it creates your reality is the first step towards taking charge of your thoughts and transforming your expectations.

Become mindful of your thoughts

In order to know what you're really thinking and how this impacts on your sense of self and your expectations, its important to develop an awareness of the thoughts that are constantly running through your mind. If you make a conscious decision to monitor your thoughts, you'll almost certainly find that there are themes that are being repeated over and over again. In Buddhism, the term 'monkey mind' is used to describe the constant chattering of thoughts that occupy our minds. We literally think thousands of thoughts a day and most of them are repetitive. What we focus on expands, and so these recurring thoughts continually reinforce our reality by affirming what we believe to be true. Negative thoughts are particularly insidious, because they often tend to be unconscious.

Even though we aren't always aware of the accumulated thoughts and beliefs that clutter our subconscious minds, they have the power to affect our moods and how we feel about ourselves. Positive thoughts create a sense of well-being, optimism and trust. Negative thoughts can manifest as vague feelings of discontent, chronic self-criticism or nagging self-doubt. They are also toxic to the body and can make us feel exhausted, lethargic or even unwell, as they drain us of our energy and vitality. Thoughts also impact on our body language and affect our posture and facial expression. When we are gripped by a negative thought we drop our heads and round our shoulders – we collapse into ourselves. Positive thoughts literally uplift and energise us.

> positive thoughts create a sense of well-being, optimism and trust

Fearful thinking

Another negative thought pattern that we can easily fall into is fearful thinking. When we are in this mode we anticipate the worst possible outcome. Here are some examples of fearful thinking:

- What if my heart gets broken?
- What if my relationship ends?
- What if there's nobody out there for me?

It's quite remarkable how much of this fearful thinking we fall into and how debilitating it is to our emotional well-being. And when our energy becomes depleted in this way, we fail to attract anything positive into our lives. Worse than that, when you feel fearful, for example, of being on your own or of your ability to maintain a relationship, it can become a self-fulfilling prophecy. And you end up experiencing the very thing that you are most afraid of.

Fearful thinking arises when we don't feel safe. This may have its roots in our early years when our environment felt threatening to our security and well-being. A parent might have left or died, or was unable to take care of all of our basic needs. This sets up a pattern of fear that prevents us from being able to trust in others. We inevitably relive the past in our present relationship patterns until we have made these conscious. An earlier heartbreak that we experienced either as a child or as an adult can powerfully influence our choices and experiences in the here-and-now but they always give us the opportunity for healing. It can take time to heal the part of us that lives on red alert. It means that we must begin to take very good care of ourselves so that we learn to trust our own resources and ability to love and look after our needs. When you begin that process, you can gradually replace your fearful expectations and learn to expect the best. This takes practice, but it will dramatically change your experience and enable you to create a loving and trusting relationship.

Discover your inner critic

Do you often blame or criticise yourself for what happens in your life? If the answer is yes, you are in the grip of your 'inner critic'. That's the voice inside you that is always telling you that you've got it wrong or should have done it differently. Your inner critic will always find fault with you, and if it has a strong enough hold on you it will make it impossible for you to feel good about yourself or feel deserving of a loving relationship. Self-blame is tantamount to being your own judge and jury, and finding yourself guilty as charged. It is corrosive and self-defeating to be so hard on yourself, so it's important to recognise how devaluing this is.

You devalue yourself when you think that you aren't good enough and choose not to see what is unique and special about you and when you sacrifice yourself and your own needs. When you devalue yourself and put yourself down, you are unlikely to be valued by others. In fact, you are more likely to attract the same kind of treatment from a partner as you give to yourself, which will further reinforce your feelings of worthlessness and inadequacy. Your life, your experience and what the world reflects back to you all mirror how you feel about your own value. If you want to feel good about yourself and your capacity to be in a good relationship, it's absolutely essential to shift from criticising and devaluing yourself to acknowledging your value and what's good about you and your life right now. It is your sense of self-value which ultimately enables you to attract someone of similar value. If you want to attract your perfect partner, you need to let yourself be a perfect partner too. This doesn't mean that you both have to attain perfection. It simply means that you are perfectly suited.

> it's essential to shift from criticising yourself to acknowledging your value and what's good about you

---

 **brilliant** action

- Next time your 'inner critic' comes up with a negative statement, replace it with a more loving and positive affirmation.

- Become aware of what you think of yourself by how you act and by how others act towards you.

- When you catch yourself in a situation which makes you aware of your lack of self-value, such as going into sacrifice, distracting yourself by keeping endlessly busy or numbing yourself in some way make a new decision about yourself.

Be kind to yourself

Are you critical and judgemental of your partner? However hard you are on others will invariably reflect how hard you are on yourself. So first and foremost, you need to start practising being kind to yourself and showing yourself some love and compassion. Go back to Chapter 1 and look at all the suggestions for how to enjoy 'being' time. Notice any resistance you may have to this and whether your inner critic attempts to undermine you. Gently tell it that, in spite of all the reasons it has to try to make you feel bad about yourself, you are choosing to feel good by doing loving things for yourself.

brilliant tip

When we take good care of ourselves we learn to trust our own resources and ability to look after our own needs.

From negative to positive thinking

The good news is that we can break the vicious cycle of negative thinking and low expectations, and affirm to ourselves that, no matter what we have been told or tell ourselves, we are lovable and deserving of love. And we can do this by changing our thinking and adopting positive beliefs about our ability to create

happy and fulfilling relationships. Whatever we affirm to ourselves on a repeated basis becomes our truth.

 action

Take a look at the following affirmations and see if you can add some of
your own. First state a negative belief you might have, and then change it
into a positive one.

Thoughts that inhibit a loving relationship	Thoughts that attract a loving relationship
I don't deserve love	I deserve a loving relationship
I have to earn love	I am lovable just as I am
I can never get what I really want	I have everything I need
All the people I am attracted to are taken	I can attract my perfect match
If I show myself as I really am, I will be rejected	I accept all of who I am
I'll never feel attractive	I love and approve of myself
I have to do all the giving in relationships	I give and receive in equal measure
I'm afraid of feeling vulnerable	I trust myself to be open
No one will ever love me	I expect to be loved and appreciated

Our negative beliefs can clearly inhibit our capacity to attract
and enjoy a loving relationship and they can be quite persist-
ent. In spite of the pain that they cause, they become part of our
identity – our comfort zone. When we challenge these limiting
beliefs about love and relationships, we move out of our comfort
zone and begin to open ourselves up to a completely different
and much more fulfilling way of being in a relationship.

To develop positive self-belief, you need to:

● value your uniqueness and not compare yourself with others;

- be true to yourself;
- commit to your own happiness;
- support yourself and back your own decisions;
- always take responsibility for your own happiness;
- check that your thoughts are supportive and affirming of you;
- acknowledge how far you've already come;
- develop your innate resources and talents;
- practise an attitude of gratitude.

brilliant tip

Whatever we affirm to ourselves on a repeated basis becomes our truth.

Develop an attitude of gratitude

Many of us fall into the trap of not appreciating the positives in our lives and instead focusing on what is missing. This makes us feel discontented and dissatisfied with our lives. When you develop an attitude of gratitude you feel more positive, satisfied, energised and optimistic. You also reduce your stress levels and take control of your own happiness. When you make a conscious choice to see the good that already exists in you and your life, it has a tremendous impact.

- On a psychological level you are likely to experience positive emotions and feel much more open, energised and productive.
- Physically, you'll begin to feel much more positive about your health, your body and your well-being.
- You can expect to experience greater joy and satisfaction in your relationships, as you experience more connection to other people.

The quality of our relationships is one of the biggest contributing factors to our happiness and well-being. An attitude of gratitude helps us to appreciate our important relationships and makes us feel affirmed and valued. Making gratitude a part of your daily life can radically change your perspective and expectations and give you a new lease of life. Instead of focusing on discontent, deprivation and disappointment, you start to put your attention on and create a feeling of abundance. As you experience the benefits of being grateful for what you already have, you begin to develop a joyful anticipation and expectation of what else is possible.

brilliant tip

When you develop an attitude of gratitude you feel more positive and optimistic. You also reduce your stress levels and take control of your own happiness.

brilliant action

Make a list of everything that you are grateful for. Remind yourself of all the gifts and good things you enjoy. These can be personal attributes, possessions or valued people in your life. Start with five and see if you can add more examples. If nothing comes to mind, think about the things that you take for granted, such as the food you eat each day or your health.

I am grateful for:

1

2

3

4

5

Focus on your gratitude list when you wake up in the morning and before you go to sleep at night. As your energy and expectations expand, you may notice that you spontaneously find other times in the day when you feel inspired to focus on what you are grateful for.

Take responsibility for your happiness

One of the most dramatic changes that you can make to feel good about who you are and create a brilliant relationship is to take complete responsibility for your happiness and the quality of your relationships. When you expect others to make you happy, you set yourself up for inevitable disappointment. And you're more likely to blame them if they fail to deliver the happiness you expect of them. When you blame others you become resentful, stuck and disempowered and abdicate responsibility for your own happiness. Needless to say, this strategy doesn't work, as playing the victim doesn't make you happy. And it certainly doesn't enable you to give and receive love.

So if you are feeling hard done by, it's time to start changing your thinking and seeing yourself as the sole creator of your happiness – no matter what your experiences have been up until now. This takes courage and time, but only *you* can make it happen.

> it's time to start changing your thinking and seeing yourself as the sole creator of your happiness

Begin by being open to acknowledging the part that you play in creating your experiences. As you become more aware of the contribution you make to your own happiness, you shift from feeling powerless to feeling powerful. Taking responsibility for your own happiness means that you stop hoping and waiting for something – or someone – to change. You come to terms with the fact that your happiness depends on you. And you begin to learn the importance of valuing yourself for who you are and what you have to offer in a relationship.

Remember you are unique

When we don't love and value ourselves we are unable to appreciate what is unique and special about us. We compare ourselves with others and find ourselves lacking. It's impossible to have a healthy relationship with yourself, when you never feel like you're measuring up. And you'll inevitably have very low expectations of attracting a good relationship or being happy in your current one. The truth is that if you are unique then you are also incomparable. And when you truly appreciate who you are, you can expect others to do the same.

 **action**

What makes you unique? You may find it hard to come up with a lot of examples at first, so start with one or two and gradually add to your list. Enjoy the process of acknowledging what's special about you.

What's unique about me?

1

2

3

4

5

 **example**

Transform your expectations

When I first met Ramon he was feeling very despondent about his relationship. He had been with Chrissie for a year and although they still felt attracted to each other and enjoyed aspects of their relationship, Ramon could feel that she was pulling away and not wanting to spend so much time together.

Ramon admitted that this was a recurring pattern in his relationships and that his partners had all ended up leaving him. When we explored this very painful theme in his life, it became apparent that he carried a powerful expectation that relationships never last and that his partners would inevitably get bored or fed up with him and move on. The template for this pattern originated in Ramon's childhood and he began to see how his very early experiences had affected every intimate relationship he had been in.

As Ramon began to consciously work on healing his early wounding and change his negative expectations to positive ones, his relationship with Chrissie changed for the better. Some time later he contacted me and told me that they had decided to live together, were very happy and thinking about starting a family.

Ignorance is not bliss

Whatever your experiences have been in relationships, the one common denominator is you. Taking a long hard look at yourself requires courage and determination. Not surprisingly, many feel unequal to the task of self-examination and choose to remain ignorant. But this is certainly not a blissful state to be in. In fact, it is much more likely to cause a serious amount of pain, disappointment and frustration. Relationship challenges don't magically resolve themselves. And hoping that your perfect partner will just show up is leaving a lot to chance. So think about the role you play in your own happiness. Then you can begin to create the love and fulfilment you desire.

 **brilliant** recap

Your beliefs and expectations have a profound impact on the quality of your relationships. When you become aware of these you can begin to change the ones that undermine you and your ability to be happy, and so create more loving and fulfilling relationships.

brilliant task for the week

Think of one negative belief that you have and then think of as many positive affirmations as you can to change it.

CHAPTER 3

Become a great communicator

The way we communicate with others and with ourselves ultimately determines the quality of our lives.

Anthony Robbins, motivational speaker

Communication is one of the greatest joys of a relationship. In fact, successful relationships rely and grow on honest and open communication. When this is lacking or absent, relationships fail to thrive and invariably drift apart. There are many ways in which we communicate and each of us has our own individual style and approach. Even if you and your partner have a very different way of expressing yourselves, when you communicate well you create rapport and build bridges that turn differences and conflicts into mutual understanding and respect. Good communication isn't a given, it's a skill – and when mastered it will enhance and stimulate your relationship immeasurably.

When you become a good communicator you discover what it is to be truly connected with your partner and experience the joy of being totally in tune with each other's thoughts and feelings. Best of all, becoming a good communicator will enable your love to deepen and grow, as you and your partner develop mutual trust and understanding and learn to express yourselves authentically, freely and openly.

Being a good communicator means:

- being able to express your opinions and feelings in an open, honest way;
- saying clearly what you mean and meaning what you say;
- building rapport by smiling and nodding to confirm you are truly listening;
- being willing to listen respectfully to each other, even if you have different perspectives;
- asking open-ended questions;
- feeling heard;
- maintaining eye contact;
- understanding and accepting each other's feelings;
- never assuming that you know better than your partner what they mean.

Why do we communicate the way we do?

The level of fulfilment or frustration that exists between you and others will to a large extent depend on:

- how easily and openly you are able to express yourselves;
- how well you listen to each other;
- how willing you are to bridge any differences between you.

For all kinds of reasons, our ability or willingness to perform these deceptively simple tasks is often lacking. That's because we don't always trust ourselves to say what we think or feel. We often doubt ourselves and lack the confidence to say what's really going on for us. Equally, if we didn't experience good communication growing up, we can be mistrustful of others and not feel safe enough to reveal ourselves to them. This can be expressed as narcissistic tendencies in which we aren't able to relate well and are more focused on ourselves than the other person.

In part, our way of relating and communicating is a reflection of our personality. Some of us are natural extroverts and confidently believe in always being open and honest. And some of us are more introverted, reserved and cautious in how we communicate. Many of us have a complex mix of being open in some situations and closed in others. But no matter what mould you seem to be set in, the good news is that you can transform the way in which you communicate and dramatically enhance the level of connection and rapport in your relationships.

> our way of relating and communicating is a reflection of our personality

A powerful influence in the way in which we communicate comes from our early experiences. In particular, the way in which our parents communicated with us – and each other – will have had a strong influence on our approach to communication and either helped or hindered us to find our own voice. For example, if you are inherently forthright with a tendency to speak your mind and this was encouraged in your childhood, you will almost certainly feel comfortable being open and expressing your natural style. But if you were reprimanded or criticised for your directness, you may have lost the confidence and trust in yourself to speak your truth. Hand in hand with this comes an expectation that others won't be interested in what you have to say.

You may not be conscious of how these early patterns operate or how they impact on the way in which you engage in your adult relationships. But you can be sure that they do. So what happens when you lose the confidence to communicate what you're really thinking and how you're really feeling? When you hold back from communicating openly and honestly and mask your true thoughts and feelings, you deny yourself the opportunity of having a real and authentic dialogue. And when two people are pretending to be something they're not, it will be impossible for them to feel loved and appreciated for who they are.

So, how do you build the confidence to express yourself authentically and trust that your partner will hear what you're saying?

 **brilliant** example

Engage with your partner and create an authentic connection

Jonathan grew up in a large family. He was the youngest of four children and all his siblings had strong and assertive personalities. Neither of Jonathan's parents had a lot of time for him; his father was often away on business and his mother was too busy to give Jonathan the attention that he needed. Jonathan never felt that he could speak up for what he wanted and so he learned to keep quiet and not make any trouble. In his adult relationships Jonathan re-enacted his childhood pattern. He attracted women who were emotionally distant and who never really seemed that interested in him. As a result, he remained closed and uncommunicative. The one time that he did meet someone who showed an interest in him, she complained that he wasn't demonstrative and didn't allow himself to share his thoughts and feelings.

After I'd been working with Jonathan for a few sessions his true personality began to emerge. His warmth, humour and intelligence were just a few of the highly engaging qualities that he had never expressed. Gradually he learned to value these qualities in himself. And as Jonathan grew in self-confidence, he dared to show more and more of himself and share his innermost thoughts and feelings. He had become a great communicator! And within a year he had formed a strong and happy relationship.

Active listening

The fact that we have two ears and one mouth may say something about the importance of listening. The Chinese pictogram of the verb 'to listen' is made up of five parts. It translates as 'I give you my ears, my eyes, my undivided attention and my heart'.

How often have you felt that you weren't being listened to? Or maybe you're the one who has been accused of not listening. Without realising it, we often absent ourselves when in conversation with others and don't give our full attention to what the other person is saying. There are many reasons for distracting ourselves or switching off from what our partner is saying. We may:

- be preoccupied with our own thoughts and thinking about what we want to say next;
- be resistant to what we are hearing and react by interrupting or feeling angry or upset;
- shut down as a way of protecting ourselves from feeling any pain;
- simply not be interested.

Whatever the reason, not listening can be incredibly hurtful and damaging to a relationship. If we're not feeling listened to, we don't feel valued and acknowledged. Understandably, this can make us feel upset and angry and lead to a sense of disconnection and alienation from the very person we want to feel close to.

Active listening is a very powerful way of communicating. When you engage in active listening, you can dramatically improve the quality of communication between you and your partner. In active listening you:

- give your complete focus to what the other person is saying;
- listen to what the other person has to say with an open mind;
- let the other person finish before you start talking;
- maintain eye contact;
- demonstrate open and relaxed body language;

- reflect back what you have heard so that there are no misunderstandings;
- keep your emotions under control;
- don't interrupt or jump to conclusions;
- look for the feelings or intent behind the words.

 **tip**

When you actively listen to someone and give them your undivided attention, they will feel acknowledged and valued. This will dramatically improve the communication between you.

When you actively listen to your partner they in turn will have more attention available for you. This opens up the possibility of a real and respectful exchange in which you give each other permission to express your feelings, thoughts, needs and position. Active listening doesn't mean that you always agree with each other. It simply means that you understand – or ask for clarification if you don't – and acknowledge what your partner is saying. Active listening also helps you to create empathy and come to an agreement. You are much more likely to be receptive to what the other person is saying if you feel you have been heard and acknowledged. Active listening can also defuse a potentially explosive situation and enable you to find a constructive solution. It's unrealistic to think that we will always have a straightforward, engaging conversation in which we agree with each other all the time. If, however, you express what you want or feel while respecting the needs and different perspectives of the other person you will create the basis for a strong and supportive relationship.

 **action**

Next time you have a conversation, monitor how actively you are listening.

● Are you giving this person your undivided attention?

● If not, what is preventing you from doing so?

● Is this a pattern that you recognise?

● What feelings are coming up for you?

● Is there a difference in the way you and the other person relate to each other when you are both actively listening? If so, what is it?

At first you will need to make a conscious effort to monitor how actively you are listening, but in time this will become second nature. The more you practise active listening, the better your communication will be. And the more fulfilling your relationships will become.

What messages are you giving out?

It's not always your partner's words that you need to be able to tune into and receive. We're also receiving a lot of cues and information non-verbally. A warm embrace can say more than a thousand words. Smiling and affectionate touching communicates our positive feelings and have a reassuring and uplifting effect. The tone of voice that you adopt is also a strong indicator of how you are treating each other. Depending on your mood and temperament, this can vary from cold, angry, hostile, dictatorial and submissive to loving, kind, warm and soothing. You can literally change the quality of your interaction by changing the tone of voice in your communication.

Your tone of voice and your body language give vital clues about how you're really feeling. If you are expressing what's really true for you, your non-verbal communication and your words will match. But sometimes our words and our tone of voice don't match. For example, how many times have you or your partner said you're fine or that something doesn't matter but the tone of your voice, your facial expression and your body language have belied your words? Your body and words should say the same thing. When your words and feelings aren't congruent, you are in conflict with yourself and, consequently, you will give out a mixed message.

 **brilliant** action

If you find yourself saying one thing but feeling another, ask yourself the following questions:

● Am I reluctant/afraid to tell the truth?

● What do I imagine will happen if I do?

● What happens when I don't express how I really feel/what I really think?

● What am I avoiding by withholding my true thoughts/feelings?

● Am I in a relationship with someone who encourages me to express myself?

● Am I with someone who doesn't give me the space to be me?

● What do I need in order to be open about myself?

Question your assumptions

Without realising it, we often make quite a few assumptions about people when we first meet them. Even when you are sitting opposite a total stranger you will probably be assuming things about them, such as their age, social class and characteristics, without asking any questions. How many times have you been to a party, been introduced to someone and assumed certain things about them because of the way they dressed or spoke, only to discover that they didn't match your assumption of them at all? Or how often have you wrongly assumed something about your partner? When we make blanket assumptions they can:

- cloud our response to someone;
- reflect and reinforce our prejudices;
- lead us to misjudge people and situations;
- block us from getting to know and forming relationships with new people;
- stop us being open and curious;
- make us complacent or rigid;
- prevent us from developing as people;
- prevent our relationship from growing.

When you question your assumptions, you become more open and curious, and this enhances the quality and scope of your communication. Rather than thinking that you know all about someone, you begin to discover that there's much more to this person than you realised.

Keep noticing whether you are making any assumptions about your partner or someone that you meet for the first time. Get curious. Be willing to be surprised. Go beyond your assumptions and see what opens up.

brilliant action

If you have been in a relationship for a long time and got stuck in a rut with your partner, it will take time to discover all your assumptions about each other. Write a list of all the things that you assume about your partner. Are they really true? What assumptions do you think your partner has made about you? How do these affect the way in which you communicate? Commit to re-evaluating each assumption and notice what happens.

See conflict as a way to transform your relationship

Sooner or later we all get into conflict with our partners. This can be over simple decisions like who puts the rubbish out to more serious questions regarding our needs and what's important to us as individuals. Avoiding conflict doesn't resolve anything. In fact it is more likely to exacerbate the problem. Conflict, properly handled, can be a tool for growth and greater awareness. We need conflict in order to define ourselves and our individuality and know what is important to us.

> we need conflict in order to define ourselves and our individuality

Any unresolved conflict that you experience in yourself will inevitably manifest in your relationships. For example, if you are ambivalent about being in a committed relationship but you haven't owned up to it, this will undoubtedly get played out with your partner. For example, you might express your ambivalence by being away a lot on business or by overly asserting your independence. Or if you're not conscious of your ambivalence, your partner might act it out for you and be partly unavailable in some way. Needless to say, this is likely to cause a certain amount of friction and unhappiness in your relationship. Becoming aware of our inner conflicts enables us to resolve the issues that we do battle over.

When you are confident about who you are and where you stand you will want to communicate assertively rather than submissively or aggressively. Being assertive doesn't mean that you have to be loud but you do need to make yourself heard. If we allow the other person's needs, opinions or judgements to become more important than our own, we may end up feeling hurt, angry and frustrated. It is therefore important to express yourself clearly and authentically and aim for a win–win outcome.

 **action**

Think about any areas of conflict between you and your partner. Have you experienced similar conflicts in previous relationships? If so, then the common denominator is you. Spend some time listing the main areas of conflict in your relationships and ask yourself how these might reflect unresolved issues in you. Write down your thoughts and feelings.

1

2

3

4

5

Take responsibility for your feelings

What often happens when we experience conflict in our relationships is that we attempt to make the other person responsible for what we are feeling, blaming them for the situation and trying to get them to meet our needs. And rather than openly address the issue, we defend our position – which only serves to drive a deeper wedge between us and our partner. For a relationship to grow and mature, it's essential that you take responsibility for your feelings. After all, they belong to you. You will develop trust and confidence in the relationship when you don't target each other as the ogres of the piece. Owning your feelings and working through them rather than attempting to change your partner is a powerful way to transform the situation.

Step back and collect your thoughts

It's not always easy to put words to feelings or express our thoughts clearly. Sometimes we feel inarticulate and blocked. When we can't find the right words to express what we're feeling we often end up feeling frustrated. If you are experiencing difficulty in voicing what's going on inside you, take a few moments to collect your thoughts. You might even want to write them down in a journal or notebook. This will give them form and coherence and help you to express them more clearly.

Express your needs clearly

It can feel risky to express what you desire or need. But when you withhold this information you are in effect expecting your partner to be a mind reader. Although some people do naturally intuit the thoughts and feelings of their partner, most of us need to have these explained to us. If we really want our partner to respond to our needs, it's important to state these clearly and specifically. If you are vague about what you want or you expect your partner always to know what you need, you set yourself up for disappointment. Not only that, but your partner may feel manipulated if your needs are expressed covertly. So be specific. 'I wish I felt more loved' or 'I wish we could spend more time together' aren't direct enough to change anything. Here are some examples of expressing your needs more directly.

- 'I need you to be more demonstrative with your feelings.'
- 'I need us to spend more time together.'
- 'I'd like you to call me if you're going to be late.'

And remember, this is not about blame. It's about being clear about what you want and expressing this openly. It's also about resolving issues and changing habits or patterns that don't support you or the relationship.

Don't allow things to build up

Sometimes we adopt the belief that it's better to keep the peace rather than express how we're feeling. The problem with this strategy is that it's usually a fear-based response to a situation that we are afraid to confront. For example, we might worry that by daring to speak our truth we'll open up a can of worms or unleash a very strong reaction which we won't be able to handle. However, the uncomfortable feelings that we try so hard to suppress don't go away. They slowly fester and can gradually build to an intolerable level of anger and resentment. When this happens, you either end up expressing anger inappropriately or you are left with a profound sense of impotence. This not only has a hugely detrimental effect on your relationship, but also on your physical and emotional well-being.

State your grievances in the present

If you are unhappy about something that your partner has just said or done, try to address this at the time. When grievances accumulate, you'll probably overreact when you do finally acknowledge how you're feeling. Not only that, but when you bring up all the previous occasions in which your partner has annoyed or upset you, this will only serve to put your partner on the defensive. Instead, state in as clear and as honest a way as possible how you are feeling in the present moment and only deal with the current issue. Once you are able to resolve the current issue, you will create a more receptive space in which to discuss any past grievances.

Healthy anger

We are often afraid of our own anger or of the anger of others. Anger can be destructive when acted out inappropriately, but when it is correctly expressed it can motivate and empower

anger can actually make you think more clearly

you. Rather than make you irrational, anger can actually make you think more clearly. If you are feeling angry, it's important to avoid shaming or blaming your partner. However tempting it is to do this, especially if you feel wronged, starting a conversation with 'You always/never...' will almost certainly create more hostility between you and your partner. Rather than make your partner wrong, take responsibility for how you're feeling and start your conversation with 'I'. For example:

● 'I feel very uncomfortable when you change the subject.'

● 'I am feeling upset about the fact that you seem very distant at the moment.'

● 'I'm hurt that you spoke disparagingly about me in front of our friends.'

It's much easier to resolve any issues between you and your partner when each person owns their feelings. It's also important to recognise the part that you each play in creating the situation you find yourselves in. When you are both willing to take responsibility for your feelings and the dynamic that exists between you, you have the ingredients for an honest and authentic relationship.

brilliant action

Next time your partner says or does something that has an impact on you, try the following. State clearly: 'When you said/did that, I felt ...'. Say this without reproach or expectation. Your partner simply listens without jumping in either to fix the situation or to defend themselves. Tell your partner what you need from them in that moment, and explore how that feels for both of you. Be willing to explore what has happened and reach an understanding of each other's position – and, if necessary, a compromise.

 **example**

Say how you really feel

Colin and Susannah had a close, loving relationship and had been together for four years when I met them. Susannah had recently started a high-powered job and was spending longer at work as a result. Colin worked from home and, although he understood that Susannah needed to work longer hours on occasion, he was beginning to resent the fact that he never knew what time she'd be home. At first, he repressed his feelings. Rather than express his frustration with Susannah's erratic hours and constant exhaustion, he tried to be supportive. But his body language and his behaviour contradicted his words and told a different story. This annoyed Susannah and eventually the atmosphere between them became tense and hostile. When Susannah arrived home very late one evening Colin flew into a rage. Susannah was deeply hurt and upset by Colin's reaction. They had reached an impasse and both felt upset and disappointed in each other.

But when we discussed their situation it became apparent that they wanted to find a solution. I suggested that they both be very clear in communicating their feelings and needs. Their drama could have been avoided if Colin had said right at the beginning how he really felt about what was happening. Although this may not have changed the commitment that Susannah had to proving herself at work, she acknowledged that she would have been more sympathetic to how Colin was feeling and this would have helped them to reach some kind of agreement or compromise. They agreed to communicate much more clearly and openly with each other and their relationship went from strength to strength as a result.

Be authentic

Being able to express yourself authentically and knowing that your partner is willing and able to do the same sets the foundation for a fulfilling relationship. This can only be achieved when you both have confidence and trust in yourselves, and feel secure enough to be open and honest. Communication then becomes a two-way process of openness, vulnerability and acceptance, through both words and body language. Make a commitment to yourself and your partner to express your thoughts and feelings rather than cover them up or disregard them. This may feel daunting at first, so start by simply stating your joint intention to communicate more clearly and bring any issues out into the open. Failing to mention what is really important to you or what is gnawing away at you doesn't value you or the relationship. Being open and willing to share does.

Your shared goal also needs to include a commitment to respecting one another's truth. At times it can be challenging to take on board what our partner really feels and thinks. And this can often be the make-or-break point in a relationship. Revealing all can force us to confront what isn't working and what needs to change. However, when you both pledge to being truthful and respectful, your reward will be an authentic, loving, honest and respectful relationship.

 **brilliant** tip

Communication is a two-way process of openness, vulnerability, respect and acceptance.

brilliant recap

However well intended we might be, we can all fall into the trap of not communicating clearly. When you commit to practising the optimum ways in which to communicate on a daily basis, you will transform your relationships. If you are willing to engage in an open and honest dialogue then you can create the foundation for a deeply fulfilling and life-enhancing connection with your partner.

brilliant task for the week

Practise being open and sharing one thought or feeling with your partner on a daily basis. Use the techniques you have learned in this chapter to facilitate your interaction.

CHAPTER 4

Breaking up and moving on

There are things that we don't want to happen but have to accept, things we don't want to know but have to learn, and people we think we can't live without but have to let go of.

Anonymous

When we fall in love we invest all of our hopes and dreams in our beloved, we give our hearts away and invest huge amounts of time and energy in our partnerships. We want our love to last for ever. So it's no wonder that relationship break ups can be one of the most painful and traumatic events in our lives. Even when our expectations are hopelessly unrealistic, we can still feel deeply disappointed and hurt when our partner doesn't meet our needs or make us happy. Waking up one day and realising that you don't feel the same about your partner any more and that you no longer want to be with that person can be a devastating realisation. Equally, if not more, painful is hearing from your partner that they are ending the relationship.

Regardless of who initiates the break up, both parties can feel a terrible sense of failure and guilt as well as anger and deep sadness when a relationship falls apart. It takes honesty and courage to admit that your relationship is no longer working. If you are able to handle the break up with maturity and equanimity, learn the lessons and graciously wish each other well and move on, you can save yourself a lot of pain and suffering. More often than not, however, a break up is experienced as hugely traumatic and can bring out the worst in a couple. The fall out can last a long time and we won't fully recover and move on unless or until we are willing to accept what has happened and take responsibility for the part we have played.

What's important to know right from the start is that whether you delivered or received the news that your relationship is no longer tenable, and as hard as it is to come to terms with, this has happened because on some level you are no longer a match. Maybe you've outgrown each other, maybe you never really were that compatible, maybe one of you has fallen for someone else, or maybe the relationship has simply run its course. Initially, we may resist this realisation and each of us will need to process the break up of a relationship in our own way and in our own time. However, there are guidelines which can help to navigate this rocky terrain and help you to minimise your heartache and maximise your courage to heal and move on. Staying in a relationship that has run its course is a waste of precious time and energy. Ultimately, that time and energy can be spent learning the lessons of the past and help you become available for someone who is much better suited to you.

> staying in a relationship that has run its course is a waste of precious time and energy

The challenge of change

Most of us aren't comfortable with change and tend to cling to the familiar. We're creatures of habit. We want things to stay the same and we become attached to what's familiar. Sometimes we hold on to things that are safe and predictable even when we know they're not good for us. Nowhere is this characteristic more apparent than in relationships. When a couple first declare their undying love for each other there's an assumption – or at least a heartfelt hope – that it will last for ever and that come what may, they will always be there for each other. That's why it can be so hard to come to terms with the fact that a relationship isn't working or has come to an end. In fact, we often protect ourselves from such a painful realisation by staying in denial about how unhappy we are and may choose to stay in a loveless, dead-end relationship rather than risk rocking the boat and facing the unknown.

We very rarely arrive at the same conclusion at the same time about the state of our relationships. It *can* happen that two people simultaneously recognise that their relationship is failing and are both willing to talk about their feelings and reconcile themselves to the fact that they've outgrown each other and then move on. A more common scenario is that the person who initiates the break up acknowledges that they have been unhappy for a while and eventually plucks up the courage to confront the situation with their partner.

When one person ends a relationship their partner can react in a number of ways. Much like the grieving process after a bereavement, these different and complex emotions can come in waves and range from denial, hurt, shock, anger, confusion, depression, resignation, sadness, panic, bewilderment to despair. If you don't feel ready or equipped to deal with a break up, you may be willing to do anything to save the situation. Anything rather than face the pain and humiliation of being rejected, left and alone.

So often the person being left insists that they never saw the break up coming, that they thought that any issues had been resolved or that they were getting along fine. There might have been disagreements and attempts to work harder at the relationship, but it can still come as a shock when you are faced with the stark reality that your relationship is over. But in truth, a happy a happy and successful relationship requires both people to be fulfilled and content

and successful relationship requires both people to be fulfilled and content. When one person doesn't feel that way, no matter how much the other person tries to turn a blind eye, they too will be unhappy deep down and know on some level that the relationship isn't working. It may appear that the break up came out of the blue but that's almost always because one person is in denial about the state of play between them and their partner. It's as if each person has been in a different relationship.

Fear is a natural part of breaking up

Each of us has different values and approaches to life and relationships and we all have varying pain thresholds. Some of us can tolerate years of unhappiness if we have low self-esteem and don't feel we deserve a better relationship. Others may feel obliged to keep working at the relationship once a commitment is made. This can come from an overdeveloped sense of duty and responsibility as well as a strong investment in the status quo. Fear also plays its part – our attachments go very deep and the separation anxiety that we experience at the prospect of a relationship ending can be crippling. Our very survival can feel at stake and although our rational selves know that we aren't literally going to die if our partner leaves us or the relationship breaks up, on an emotional level it can feel as if our lives are over and that there is nothing else beyond the pain we are feeling.

Relationships break up for different reasons

We meet someone we are deeply attracted to and we fall in love. That's the easy part. Intimate relationships bring out the best and the worst in us and challenge us in ways that other relationships don't. They can make us feel on top of the world and they can also make us feel excruciatingly vulnerable. There are no guarantees about how our relationships will end up. Sometimes we stay together and sometimes we move apart. Couples who are a good match and commit to keeping their relationship alive and making it work will learn to resolve their differences, survive the low points and develop confidence in the value of their relationship. This creates a strong bond and enables the partnership to grow and flourish. If, however, the partnership isn't able to develop in this way, the bond weakens over time and becomes more based on habit than on love. Whatever the circumstances, when two people are no longer speaking the same language they begin to see the relationship – and each other – from very different perspectives. When we have been with a partner for a long time our relationship becomes a given part of our lives so we never really stop to ask – is this the sort of relationship that I've always wanted?

 **example**

Acknowledge your part in the break up

Tom and Jasmine had been together for a few years and although their relationship worked for a while, increasingly they had become less communicative and more distant from each other. Tom's expectations were relatively low and he didn't think that he was unhappy. Jasmine, on the other hand was aware that she wanted more from a relationship and that she and Tom had drifted apart because they were fundamentally incompatible. Tom felt very threatened by Jasmine's desire to leave their relationship and in their joint coaching session he expressed anger and resentment towards her.

Jasmine did end the relationship and start a new life and Tom decided to have some individual sessions to help him get some perspective and clarity on where he found himself. As he began to take responsibility for

▶

his part in the break up and realised that he hadn't been happy either, he became less angry towards Jasmine and more understanding of why things hadn't worked out between them. Ultimately this enabled him to gain a deeper awareness of his relationship patterns and create a much happier relationship with someone else.

There are many ways to end a relationship and none of them are easy. A complex number of factors are involved to reach such a decision. The way in which your relationship ends will depend on your individual personalities, the state of play between you and your partner and what you both expect from your partnership. If a relationship has endured years of unhappiness and countless attempts to try harder which went nowhere, it can be frustrating and disheartening when one partner cannot see that the relationship is over. When differences can no longer be reconciled, it's better to cut our losses and put an end to the unhappiness of being in a relationship which is no longer happy or fulfilling. But what happens when one person wants another chance or angrily demands to know why the relationship is over? If you have initiated a break up and your partner is in denial, you may need to be patient until they come to terms with what's happened. One symptom of denial is doing everything you can to procrastinate and delay the inevitable.

Shock is a natural reaction to traumatic news and it takes time to sink in – even if the relationship has been unhappy for several years. In the beginning – and perhaps for some time afterwards – there can be desperate attempts to save the relationship and downplay it or dismiss the unwelcome news. If you aren't in step with your partner's desire to end the relationship you may hope against hope that your partner doesn't mean it or is exaggerating the problem and that it will therefore go away. But this will only exacerbate the problem. This may sound glib but a lot of the pain you are experiencing right now is actually fear. Fear of being out of your comfort zone, fear of being alone, fear of never finding another partner, fear of being thrown out of your routine and not knowing how you're going to spend your time and fill the empty space.

Make sense of what has happened

Focusing on a bleak future which may never happen disempowers you and doesn't help you to deal with the here and now. There's no quick fix for the heartache of a break up and for a while at least, you will need to be very kind and compassionate with yourself as you adjust to your new situation and make sense of what has happened. This means taking it slowly, breathing deeply and reminding yourself that no matter how low your self-esteem might be right now, you are still a lovable and amazing person. Nothing can change that. And when you hold on to that reality and find the courage and good grace to be open and courageous in how you respond to your break up, your future will begin to look a lot brighter.

It's natural to want to find solutions to problems and this may be the first reaction you have to a break up. It's important at this stage to be willing to get a sense of what has happened without trying to fix anything. Really listen to your partner – hear what is being said. Engage with them even if you find it hard to hear what they have to say. Find out how long they have felt that way and what prompted their decision. Reflect back to them your understanding of what they have said so that you can start to clarify in your own mind where you find yourselves. When you are willing to listen to your partner they are more likely to be open to hear how you're feeling and in that way you can open up a constructive dialogue. Good com-

> when you are willing to listen to your partner they are more likely to be open to hear how you're feeling

munication depends on both parties being willing to be open and honest. If this isn't the case and one person wants to raise issues while the other wants to keep a lid on things, the problems become more and more ingrained.

 **brilliant** action

If you still cannot understand why your relationship has ended/is ending, try this exercise of looking back with a renewed perspective.

● If you were really honest with yourself, what part did you play in the break up of your relationship?

● When did you notice that things started to go wrong?

Take a piece of paper and draw a line down the middle. On one side of the paper write 'My responsibility' and on the other side write 'My partner's responsibility'. Start with your partner and list all the ways in which you believe they contributed to the break up. Notice how you're feeling and breathe through any difficult feelings. Next list your contributing factors for the break up.

This can be a challenging exercise, especially if you don't recognise how you played your part or you are intent on blaming your partner. It's impossible to be objective but as much as possible, try to detach from any strong emotion and just write everything you can think of. The clearer your perspective is, the more easily you will be able to reconcile yourself with what happened and move on with your life. Be kind and patient with yourself.

Accept your part but don't blame yourself

When emotions are running high it's impossible to communicate clearly. Wait until you and your partner are feeling calmer before you agree to talk about your break up. Take it in turns to speak and really listen to your partner and try to accept that his or her feelings are valid. It might initially be comforting to think it's not your fault and that either circumstances or the other person is to blame, but in the long term, playing victim makes it hard to learn from your experience, grow, move on and find someone new. If you feel hard done by in your relationship and the way that it ended, this leaves you vulnerable to repeating a pattern.

It's easy to get into blame when a relationship breaks up. Sometimes one party has clearly crossed a line and this may well have contributed to the demise of your relationship. Or perhaps you were the one who behaved badly and you reproach yourself for that. Ultimately, both of you will have played a part in how you conducted your relationship and how it turns out. Even when it appears as if one party is the villain of the piece, the other person will have colluded in some way with their behaviour.

Taking responsibility for your part in the relationship doesn't mean going into self-blame. It means being honest with yourself and seeing how you contributed to the way in which your relationship unfolded. Of course you may decide that if you had a second chance you would do certain things differently. There are always lessons to be learned. These lessons, and the awareness that you gain about yourself and your relationship dynamic will almost certainly inform the way you go into the next relationship and give you a clearer perspective on what you do and don't want next time. But resist the temptation to feel bad about yourself. When you feel bad about yourself you replay the same old scenarios in your head. For instance, you may replay wonderful moments that you had together and convince yourself that you did something wrong to make those wonderful moments stop happening. This leads to going over mistakes that you believe you made and devaluing yourself with negative beliefs like, 'If only I'd ... this wouldn't have happened and we'd still be together'. You think about what you could have said or should have done and all this does is make you feel worse than you're already feeling. If you start to undermine yourself in this way when you go over what happened in your relationship, make a conscious decision to not berate yourself or make your anger and disappointment all about what your partner did or didn't do. Instead, take a step back and consider the following questions.

 **action**

Without blaming yourself or your partner, be as honest as you can and ask yourself:

- What have you done or not done that has contributed to the outcome?
- If you could do it all again, what would you do differently?
- Are any of your partner's complaints justified? If so, which ones?
- Were any of your expectations of your partner and the relationship unrealistic? If so, which ones?
- What can you learn from your experience? In which way does this learning enable you to grow in self-awareness, heal and move on?

Keep a journal

Often, when faced with a challenge we discover resources and strengths that we didn't know we had. However, sometimes our situation seems so bleak that our coping mechanisms are overwhelmed. When that happens, we go into catastrophic thinking and imagine the worst. We lose sight of the fact that we are intelligent and resourceful and that when push comes to shove we can find the wherewithal to deal with our situation, no matter how distressing it feels. When you feel yourself being overwhelmed by sadness, pain or negativity, try committing those feelings to paper. Keeping a journal can be very cathartic and therapeutic and a wonderful way to connect with and understand your emotions. It will also help you communicate better with your partner when you are discussing your break up.

 **brilliant** action

Either in your journal or on a separate piece of paper, complete the following sentence and write down all the implications. Give yourself free rein and allow all your feelings and thoughts to surface.

'If my partner and I split up ...'

If this feels too hard to do or if you feel that you need support around your break up, you might want to see a counsellor or a therapist or choose a confidante who is caring and empathetic and willing to act as a sounding board.

It's hard to fathom the exact reasons for a break up and find out what's underneath the growing apart and incompatibility. Here are some of the most common:

● betrayal of trust – secrets, infidelity and lies all severely undermine a relationship. Not all betrayals are of a romantic nature but once they occur, it can be very hard to forgive and trust again;

● children leave home and without the glue and distraction of looking after them, couples realise that there is nothing else holding them together;

● one partner may want children and the other doesn't;

● debt;

● drinking and drugs;

● jealousy;

● irritating habits;

● moodiness.

There can be other factors involved in driving two people apart. Any kind of life crisis can prompt us to review our lives and realise that our relationship has reached an impasse. We may suddenly feel a compelling sense that life is short and this can precipitate a powerful desire to take control of our lives and make significant changes. The catalyst for this could be a death, boredom at work or a growing sense that something fundamental is wrong. This realisation can have the effect of turning lives upside down and if both partners aren't in tune with these changes it can create a gulf between them.

It can be very threatening for one person to feel that their partner wants to make a big life change. What's at the root of this concern is often the fear that they will be left behind. Trying to hold someone back from growing and going his or her own way only delays the inevitable and makes it more difficult to deal with. Letting go is one of the hardest things we can do and involves a huge amount of trust. And yet there are times when we have no other choice and we simply have to trust that if the end of the relationship is right for one person, on some level it is right for both of you.

Can your relationship be saved?

Sometimes a break up is a fait accompli and there is no room for negotiation or discussion. Before reaching that stage, it can be helpful for both partners to take another look at their relationship to see whether it can be saved. Even if it proves to be a lost cause, this process can make the eventual split more of a joint decision. Depending on how you are both feeling, you may choose to do this together or with a relationship counsellor. Once you begin to process the impact of the potential break up, you might be surprised to discover that the reasons for the relationship breaking down are more complex than imagined. As you reflect on how you got to this point you may gradually be willing to finally face the problems and recognise where you are. Although it's natural to wonder whether there is any possibility of saving the relationship and still have a future together, it's important to be realistic and not harbour any false hopes. Fighting a losing battle is demoralising, draining and only prolongs the agony. It takes courage to honestly assess whether your relationship has truly run its course and a lot of goodwill and trust for you to work together in this way.

brilliant action

Have a look at the checklist below and see how many of the statements are true for you. This will help you get a clearer perspective on your relationship.

- It's very difficult to show love and affection.
- We rarely – if ever – have sex.
- A lot of our communication involves put downs, name calling and cold, dismissive or aggressive body language (arms folded, deep sighs, eye rolling and turning away).
- We no longer look forward to being together.
- We avoid any kind of emotional intimacy.
- There is no shared humour.
- One of us/both of us feel angry, resentful and upset a lot of the time.
- Any attempt to discuss problems turns into blaming, arguments and going into defence.
- The relationship feels disempowering.
- One of us/both of us are often hostile, detached or simply reluctant to engage with each other.
- We're not able to communicate without things being misinterpreted.
- One of us/both of us has changed. It doesn't feel like I'm with the person that I fell in love with.

▶

If you ticked more than four statements, your relationship is clearly not working. When we're angry and disappointed, it's easy to take our unhappiness out on each other and this behaviour leads to a downward spiral with both partners feeling justified in their recriminations. Ultimately, it takes two to make a relationship work and if there isn't enough goodwill, trust and desire to work together it can't be repaired. Being willing to accept the reality of your situation and reaching an understanding of why your relationship has come unstuck is empowering and ultimately liberating. It enables you to see what needs to change and either save the relationship or move on and make a better relationship next time.

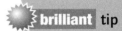 **tip**

> It takes two to make a relationship and it can't be repaired if there isn't enough goodwill, trust and desire to make it work.

Choose to see change as positive

When we're under stress – like at times of change – our brain operates differently. We go into survival mode and this means that we're less able to be cool, calm and collected and think things through. Even though a part of our brain interprets change as potentially threatening, the reality is that change is neither intrinsically good nor bad. It depends on our attitude. The stress of a break up means that you're more likely to see all the negatives about your situation. Even if deep down, some part of you is secretly relieved – especially if you have instigated the break up – there will also be some other strong emotions connected to the end of your relationship. Even the most mutual of splits can still bring up painful emotions which take time to process. If you can't see any immediate benefits to splitting up, try looking a bit further into the future and ask yourself how it might look when you're over the shock and disappointment and your life is starting to open up again. Secondly, ask yourself what would happen if things didn't change. What is the downside of staying where you are? And what is the pay off? However despondent you are feeling, remember that you are breaking free from a relationship that for whatever reason, wasn't working. And that freedom will enable you to recreate your life and give you a chance to find happiness with someone else.

 **action**

When you're in the throes of a break up it's easy to give in to self-defeating patterns. We can often neglect ourselves when we're in pain and forget to keep nurturing and nourishing ourselves with kindness, compassion, positive thoughts and healthy choices around food and exercise. Finding ways to change your state and shift into a more positive state of mind is always available to you and it's important that you find ways to relax, be in the moment, move and stay grounded.

Here are some ways to help you do that:

- Take deep breaths. When you're oxygenated you feel more alive and energised. You also think more clearly.
- Drink lots of water. This will keep you hydrated and clear headed.
- Go for a long walk in a beautiful place. Moving your body and being in nature is uplifting and energising.
- Dig the garden. It feels good to be productive and do something therapeutic.
- Listen to uplifting music.
- Spend time with supportive friends who know only too well where you are.
- Do some de-cluttering and lighten your load. This might be a good time to pack up all your photos and relationship memorabilia as these reminders can really rub salt into the wound.

▶

- Make a delicious meal or go to a great restaurant. There's nothing like quality food to make us feel comforted and nurtured. Resist the temptation to fill up on junk food. Make an effort to eat well. Your body will be grateful to you and this will make you feel good about yourself.

- Read books that inspire you. Choose books about people who have led extraordinary lives or come through major challenges. See them as role models.

- Go somewhere you've never been before or a place you've always longed to visit. It will take you out of yourself and remind you that there's a whole world out there.

- And remember, you have been through change before and come out the other side. Think back to times when you have successfully dealt with change and how much stronger and wiser you felt for it.

Reclaim yourself

When you're no longer in a relationship you go from being a 'we' to having to start thinking of yourself as an 'I'. This can be a hard adjustment to make but rather than seeing yourself as diminished in some way, think of it as reclaiming yourself and forging a new identity. There is so much more for you to discover about yourself so trust that this is the best time for you to embark on that journey. Remind yourself of all the things that you're good at, that you enjoy and that you still want to do with your life. Pick one thing that you've always wanted to do and never got around to it and do it on your own. Enjoy the sense of accomplishment that this gives you and pledge to do something for yourself every week. This will help you to forge a stronger relationship with yourself and remind you of all your talents, skills and strengths.

> remind yourself of all the things that you're good at, that you enjoy and that you still want to do with your life

Get off the roller coaster

However you get there, there comes a point when splitting up is the best or the only option. Some couples will resign themselves to this reality while others will continue to fight over who did what. This creates a huge amount of stress and emotional angst and never resolves anything. The best way to eliminate this is to stop reacting to your partner and start responding in a more detached and neutral way. This isn't always easy when you're feeling a toxic mix of emotions but it will ultimately help you to get clear about where you are and what needs to happen. Keep your communication clear, take responsibility for your part and stick to the facts. For example, 'I don't think our relationship is working and I know that is partly my responsibility' or 'I feel that it's time for us to go our separate ways', is far less emotive than 'I'm disappointed that you haven't met my expectations, I don't love you any more and I want out'. If you feel lost for words and don't know how to communicate to your partner how you are feeling, write it down. This will help you to sort out your feelings and enable you to discuss them more clearly with your partner. Use this opportunity to re-examine your relationship and be certain about your choice. If you need to know where you stand legally and financially, visit your local citizen's advice bureau or a solicitor.

Put some distance between you once you've decided to break up

Sometimes, it can appear to be kinder to let your partner down gently and give the impression that although your relationship isn't working any more, maybe someday in the future you might get back together. This will only give your partner false hopes for a future with you and delay their ability to come to terms with the break up and move on. The attachment between you can still feel very sticky at this stage and although it's tempting to slowly wean yourselves off the relationship and still spend time together talking and going over what happened, once it is really obvious that you are breaking up it's more helpful to go cold turkey. If you have children or have a house together, you will need to keep communicating but keep your communication brief and polite and do your best to co-operate.

Don't try to be friends too soon, as this is hard to pull off. It's a big leap from lover to friend and it's impossible to make the transition overnight. Even if you can't imagine not having any contact with your ex, it's essential to give yourselves some space. Everyone's situation is unique but your goal should be to impose some physical – and emotional – distance between you as this will accelerate your recovery. Not seeing each other will also help you take control and get some perspective on your break up. It's so easy to have selective amnesia at this stage, romanticise the relationship and remember only the good things. But it's important to get a balanced perspective and look at the problems that you had and how – and why – the relationship deteriorated over time.

brilliant action

Try completing the following sentences and see what comes up for you. Keep writing if thoughts and feelings come pouring out.

- Putting some distance between us is going to ...
- When I focus on all the good things about the relationship it makes me feel ...
- When I recognise that the relationship wasn't perfect and that it really is over I feel ...
- When I maintain my own space and focus on what's best for me I ...
- Even when I'm feeling my worst, I know that ...

If you've still got strong feelings for your ex it will be very tempting to want to stay in touch. For a while at least, there can be a strong need for contact even though you know that it wouldn't resolve anything or make you feel any better. In fact, it will almost certainly make you feel a lot worse. Nevertheless, the withdrawal symptoms can feel acute when we suddenly no longer have that person who we cared about in our lives. And this can sometimes lead to compulsive behaviour where we find ourselves going to a place where we know our ex might be, meeting up with mutual friends or worse, calling or leaving messages or driving past where they live to see whether they're at home. None of these activities empower you or help you to focus on moving forwards and they will inevitably make you feel bad about yourself. So each time you feel the need to act out a negative impulse or find yourself obsessing about your ex, remind yourself that it is not in your best interests and choose to do something that you know will make you *really* feel good.

 **brilliant** action

Next time you feel the need to check up on your ex or indulge in obsessive behaviour, stop and ask yourself:

- What is the pay off here?
- How does this behaviour really make me feel and what is the outcome?

Remember that these distractions are holding you back from reaching acceptance, healing and moving on. Make a conscious effort to focus on your life and your best choices. Forget your ex and do something nice for you.

Manage the day to day

Commit to doing things that keep you in the present and resist the temptation to read old love letters or play songs that you listened to together. Take the best care of yourself and put yourself in a position where you are doing everything to get through this challenging time with both your dignity and your sense of self intact. By focusing on you in a positive way and giving yourself some space you are effectively giving yourself a gift.

Projecting too far into the future and allowing yourself to be overwhelmed by the prospect of what might happen to you can be scary, so try breaking the future down into manageable chunks. Bring your focus more to the present and concentrate on the day ahead and getting through the next few weeks. Instead of becoming despondent at the prospect of empty weekends or nights alone, make arrangements to do things and don't think too far ahead. If you do want to focus on the future, think about all the positive things that you'd like to manifest and begin to make that your reality. Make sure you have at least one friend who will act as a sounding board and help you keep grounded. Focus on your things that you can change and be willing to learn about yourself. Avoid over-analysing as this creates a vicious cycle and makes you feel bad about yourself and your partner.

 **brilliant** tip

The ability to find the positives will help you move more quickly to acceptance and letting go. Sometimes laughter is the best medicine so rent some funny films and spend time with friends who have a good sense of humour.

There is light at the end of the tunnel

A break up invariably acts as a wake up call to look at yourself and make new choices about your life. Whereas before you might have been coasting along, not questioning the state of play or burying your head in the sand, suddenly everything is up for review. We cannot change what's happened so be willing to let go and forgive. With forgiveness you don't get bogged down with guilt and can move on to solving the problem. When reflecting on the relationship, make sure that you're not putting any emphasis on negative thoughts. Let go of any guilt which has a toxic effect on your mind and your body. It takes real courage to face up to what has gone wrong in your relationship and recognise that it's time to move on. You may well decide that you would have behaved differently if you had another chance. But don't waste time regretting or lamenting the past. Learn from the experience and vow to make a commitment to your own happiness and well-being.

Taking responsibility for your happiness is a big part of moving on and recognising what needs to change. It takes practice and courage to be your own person, especially when you're feeling heartbroken. And you might need to push yourself a little to adjust to your new situation. Always resist the temptation to castigate yourself because you think you didn't give enough or gave too much, stayed too long or gave up too quickly. It's out of challenging times that we can really find out what we're made of and take our power. Sometimes we need to be alone to learn those lessons, and sometimes we need to be part of a couple. Only you will know what's right for you and what life is asking of you. Trust the process and the journey and take it one day at a time. This too will pass.

 **brilliant** recap

Breaking up can be one of the most painful experiences and it takes time to come to terms with the ending of a relationship. Paradoxically, break ups can also offer us the potential to discover what we are made of, let go of limiting patterns and realise that we deserve more love and happiness than we realised. When we let go and move on we give ourselves the chance to find both ourselves and a better relationship.

brilliant task for the week

If you are going through a break up or you and your partner have already split up, commit to understanding your part and how best to resolve your differences. Be willing to listen and learn and achieve the best outcome for both of you.

CHAPTER 5

The space in between

The most profound relationship we'll ever have is the one with ourselves.
Shirley MacLaine, actress and author

We've all pinned our desire for happiness onto someone or something else. And while it may be true that being with our perfect partner would deeply fulfil our lives, if we haven't yet met that special person or we find ourselves single again we need to know how to be happy in the in-between times. I call this stage of life 'the space in between'.

Most of us have hopes and dreams that have nothing to do with a relationship. These reflect our need to fulfil our potential and be all of who we can be. Perversely, we don't always pay attention to our personal ambitions and put their fulfilment on hold. Of course there's nothing wrong with hoping, visualising and dreaming about your future happiness with a partner. As we have seen in previous chapters, this heartfelt desire can play a significant part in attracting a partner to you. But when you find yourself in the space in between all kinds of other possibilities are open to you.

Life is full of the unexpected and change is inevitable at some stage. The space in between has its challenges but it also has its successes, achievements, thrills and highlights. Whether you've been on your own for a while, have just broken up, or are starting to date, the space in between gives you the chance to find new ways of supporting yourself and flourish in your own right. It can take a while to get into your stride at this stage of life, particularly if you're not used to flying solo. But in this space we can learn about ourselves and discover our amazing resources and potential, and grow more fully into ourselves. Creating a flourishing and fulfilling life at this stage requires you to focus on what makes you feel good and how you want to spend your time. It means that you don't rely on being in a relationship to feel complete. It's not particularly helpful to dwell on romantic fantasies or live in the past when your actual life is waiting to be lived. Romance, love and companionship bring great joy to our lives but they are not the only source of happiness.

 **brilliant** tip

Romance, love and companionship bring great joy to our lives but they are not the only source of happiness.

brilliant action

Before moving on in the chapter, consider the following questions:

● What dreams do you still have for yourself that aren't dependent on having a relationship?

● What are you pinning your hopes on?

● What are your aspirations?

● Are you waiting for happiness to come along, or are you ready to make your own?

● How can you be single and have a wonderful life?

Embrace being alone

All of us have fears that can bring us out into a cold sweat such as public speaking, heights or spiders. They aren't necessarily rational, but when we are in the grip of them they can paralyse us. However, what fills many of us with real dread is the fear of being alone and not being in a relationship. The extent to which we are terrified of being alone means that we will often avoid it by settling for less and choosing partners who aren't a good match for us. Or stay in stale relationships which no longer fulfil us. When we allow our fear of being alone to control us, we get into relationships, separate or divorce and then repeat the pattern. It's a vicious cycle.

Spending a part of your life alone isn't something which needs fixing. In fact, spending time alone is as natural as being in a relationship. One is not better than the other – it simply depends on where you are in your life and which option is best for you given your current circumstances. When you resist spending time alone and wish

> spending time alone is as natural as being in a relationship

that you were in a relationship instead of being single, you miss out on all the opportunities to find different kinds of fulfilment and to grow in a way that being by yourself can offer. Being able to be alone is about being satisfied and happy as an individual no matter what. Whether this is a new experience for you or you are an old hand at navigating through life by yourself, it's worth remembering that whether you are in a relationship or not, you are with yourself more than with anyone else.

Be in your own right

Each of us is unique and regardless of our relationship to others, we remain individuals in our own right. Throughout our lives we form many different kinds of relationships with friends, lovers, partners, spouses, acquaintances and colleagues but we still remain uniquely one human being. Intimate relationships fulfil our longing to experience a sense of oneness with our beloved. They also create a wonderful space in which we can endlessly explore ourselves in the presence of another and in which we can see ourselves reflected in the other. But there are other ways in which we can connect with our deepest longings, our potential and our ability to individuate. The space in between gives us that opportunity.

Our uniqueness means that some of us are better at being on our own and cultivating our own lives than others. Those of you who recognise the value of having time to yourself will make the very best of the time you have as a single person. It may take you a little time to adjust to your new status if you have recently come out of a relationship, but if you acknowledge that the timing is right and that this is the best way forward for you, this acceptance and openness to being alone for the time being will help you to make the most of this important stage of your journey. In this chapter we will look at the different ways in which you can embrace and savour having time to yourself. Ultimately, the space in between is about asking less of others and more of ourselves.

Find your own raison d'être

So often we look to our partners to give our lives meaning and when we remove that imperative from the other person we can activate our own potential. Rather than seeing the space in between as a holding pattern until you get to your next relationship, when you decide that this stretch of your journey is exactly where you're meant to be, it gives you the opportunity to open to any neglected parts of your personality. And the wonderful thing about developing yourself in this way is that you will have more to give – and receive – in your next relationship.

If, however, you are someone who doesn't like being on your own or you have gone through a particularly difficult break up, the time in between relationships can be particularly hard. When you're no longer in a relationship it sometimes seems as if love is no longer available to you. You miss that one particular person and all the good things about that relationship. Letting go of what's familiar and loved and facing the unknown makes this experience painful. But don't let the grief give you the impression that single life is all about biting the bullet and hoping that you'll somehow get through it – it's not.

You can choose to see the space in between as something positive in which you get to fall in love with yourself and find compassion, courage and the confidence to live your life as if the most important person in your world is you. And when you 'act as if' for a while, it becomes your reality. When you meet your next partner, you will enter the relationship as a stronger and more confident version of you because you'll know that as wonderful as it is to be in a loving relationship with someone, the primary loving relationship you have is with yourself.

brilliant tip

Fantasising about the future or living in the past stops you from living your actual life. Seize the day and make the most of the here and now.

Make the adjustment

If you've been used to being part of a couple, the space in between can feel as if you're suddenly part of a different culture with a whole different set of rules. It might take you a while to adjust to a different lifestyle but you can learn. Like any new skill, this takes practice and commitment but always keep in mind that you are investing in your own happiness and well-being. And once you've adapted to the new status quo and feel open to life again, all kinds of unexpected blessings and experiences can come your way. Being single, if you embrace it, can be incredibly fulfilling and enable you to develop as a person in ways in which you had never thought possible, and in the process create an even better relationship with yourself. The irony is that the more relaxed you are about being single, the more at ease you are with others. And that makes you more magnetic to a potential new relationship when the time is right.

> being single, if you embrace it, can be incredibly fulfilling and enable you to develop as a person

Be open to your choices

One of the most wonderful aspects of being in the space in between is that there are so many lifestyle choices. You can develop a new interest or devote more energy to a passion, choose to spend more time with friends and family. If you've been single for a while, you can go on dates and see how it feels to connect with people in that way again. Or you can give yourself the time and space to step back, focus exclusively on you and expand your life in new ways. Of course the space in between is also a wonderful time to take stock of your past relationships and think about what – if anything – you would do differently next time.

Sometimes we fear that if we are independent and single, we won't have love and romance in our lives. We resist becoming independent because we're afraid that if we do so, we'll be lonely, unloved and uncared for. We fear that we'll be bored and possibly depressed, with nothing to look forward to and so we do anything that we can to avoid feeling that way. When we deny ourselves the experience of living fully in the space in between, we miss out on the joy of being in love with life. And there are so many ways in which to experience love in your life when you realise that love is not dependent on being in a relationship.

Love your life

When we fall in love, it's actually our own capacity to feel love and express it which gets triggered. Love is a quality of our own heart. Love is seeing the beauty in you and who you are and sharing your being with others. If you ever felt like you were in love without being in an intimate relationship, then you know how joyful it is to feel your own capacity for love – whether you are with someone or not. When you are in this state, you can relax about finding a new relationship because you recognise that fulfilment comes in many ways. And you'll recognise the value of developing your own interests and pursuing your dreams. When you feel wobbly – which of course everyone does at times – you find strengths and abilities that you might not have known existed if you could have automatically turned to a partner. Getting through challenging times builds resilience and your core strength and these qualities empower you to be the best you can be. Not only will this make you feel great and give you a sense of achievement, but it will also make you even more the kind of person that others are irresistibly drawn to.

> getting through challenging times builds resilience and your core strength

Loving yourself and staying open to what life is showing you creates an optimum way of being and enables you to respond to all that is good about you, your life and others. When you recognise that love is an inside job you understand that even when you go through rough times, you're committed to doing the very best you can. The space in between connects us with our needs and invites us to pay more attention to them and find ways to fulfil ourselves. So often we override our own needs when we are in a relationship and compromise what is really important to us. Being single encourages us to take care of ourselves and recognise that this is an imperative if we want to enjoy the best relationship with ourselves and with our loved ones.

Each stage of our lives offers a different lesson, a different opportunity to grow and become more self-aware. Being single can be one of the most formative experiences we can have and help us discover – and reinforce – what makes us unique and how resourceful and amazing we really are. When we have space in our lives to hear the call of our soul and what life is asking of us we can make profound shifts and move closer to our essence. If you are experiencing the blessings, challenges, opportunities and lessons of being single, know that there is a purpose to you finding yourself in this place. A purpose which you may not be able to see right now but which almost certainly has your best interests at heart.

Commit to your own happiness

Many people stay in relationships because they are afraid of being alone and letting go of what's familiar. Others recognise that it's more painful to stay with what they know than to embrace change and decide to move on. Neither choice is inherently right or wrong; it simply depends on what you want for yourself and how committed you are to your own happiness. We grow and mature in many different ways when we face the reality of our aloneness. We can then put our energy into enjoying what we have in our lives and making the most of that. When we can embrace our singleness and fully live in the space in between, even though we may not always like it, we develop aspects of ourselves that we may not have done otherwise. Sometimes we consciously choose this space and sometimes it is thrust upon us. Our challenge is to rise to the occasion and live our best lives no matter how we got to this place.

 **tip**

When we embrace our singleness we develop aspects of ourselves that we may not have done otherwise. This makes us feel great and gives us a real sense of accomplishment.

Be sure of yourself

No matter how comfortable you get with being in the space in between, there will always be friends, colleagues or family members who will try to encourage you to meet someone. They may ask you whether you really want to stay single for the rest of your life, or have ever thought of signing up for an internet dating site, or tried speed dating. If people are concerned about your single status it almost certainly says more about them than it does about you. Nevertheless, it's worth thinking about how you might respond to their line of questioning. Practise your answer so that it is authentic and upbeat. You have nothing to justify and you don't need to come across as defensive. You might choose to say that you think that time on your own is a very valuable experience for you and that you're learning a lot about yourself in the process. You might also reply, if it's true for you, that you *would* like to meet someone but that you're also having a good time living your life.

Measure your success by how you live your life

Ultimately, we need to measure how successful our lives are on who we are and what we're doing and not on who we are in a relationship with. Wishing for something you don't have while ignoring all that you do have undermines your integrity and disempowers you. The more you long for something that you don't have the more disappointed and despondent you are likely to feel. Grieving for what you lost or for what you imagine you might never have again is an important step towards letting go of the past and opening yourself up to brand new possibilities. Even if you don't want to be alone, didn't choose it and don't particularly like it right now, it's important to trust that the space in between contains gold if you are willing to dig for it. It's natural to sometimes feel down about not being in a relationship. It may seem paradoxical but it's through acknowledging the stark reality of aloneness that we can come to a place of acceptance and recognise that every one of us will experience being on our own at some point in our lives. It's what we do with it that makes the difference.

brilliant action

Here are some practical exercises for embracing the space in between:

- Give yourself permission to talk about your fears of being alone with someone you trust.

- List five things that you've accomplished on your own. It doesn't matter how small or insignificant they might seem to you, just write them down and be proud of them.

- Surround yourself with things that remind you of how lovable, cherished and valued you are.

- Make a 'space in between' vision board. Cut pictures out and words from magazines that represent what you want for your life. Put it in a place where you can see it every day.

- Brainstorm and write down all the good things you can think of about this stage in your life.

The key to happiness

Finding our perfect match and living happily ever after can be a powerful driver in our psyches and this can make it hard to surrender to singleness. We long for happiness, but we tell ourselves that we can't be happy unless we have a lover or a partner. It takes determination to free ourselves of our resistance to being alone and all our preconceived notions about being single. But it's worth changing your perspective because when you are no longer held back by limiting beliefs you give yourself the freedom to be happy. Unless we bring out our limiting beliefs and narrow perspectives about being single and replace them with something more affirming we will make ourselves unhappy and create unnecessary anguish for ourselves. Singleness encompasses so much more than the narrow perspectives that our conditioning suggest. Each time you resist buying into any negative beliefs about being single you become more open to new experiences.

Here are some examples of limiting beliefs about being by yourself:

- It's selfish to live just for yourself.
- If you're not in a committed relationship by the time you've reached a certain age, it's less likely to happen.
- If you're single, you're lonely.
- If you're single, it's because you're not slim, attractive, intelligent enough etc.
- If you're single it's because you're commitment-phobic.

 **action**

What are your assumptions and beliefs about being single? Don't edit, just brainstorm and write down everything that being single means to you.

Being single means ...

For every negative belief that you have, there's a corresponding positive. Write them down. And remind yourself of them every day.

Complete the sentence:
The wonderful aspects about being single at this point in my life are ...

When you have completed your list, buy yourself an enormous bouquet of flowers or some other treat to remind yourself of how special you are.

Choose to enjoy being single

When you are not in a relationship you often have the opportunity to discover much more about yourself and cultivate your own life, interests and friendships. You also have greater freedom inasmuch as you can make decisions without having to consult anybody else and do things that you might not consider if you were in a committed relationship. It's important to keep reminding yourself that being single does not mean that you're unlovable, undesirable or antisocial. It does not mean that there is something wrong with you. It doesn't mean that you'll end up all alone in the world. Single is simply a stage of life that we all experience. Let go of any negative beliefs and replace them with a mind-set which enhances your well-being and helps you to see the many choices that lie ahead of you when you take control of your own life. Speak positively about where you are in your life now and focus on the benefits and rewards. Celebrate the spaciousness of your diary and be grateful for the time you have for your own life.

 **tip**

Being single is as natural as being in a relationship, and you'll almost certainly experience the highs and the lows of both.

Appreciate your friends

If you're just getting the hang of being in the space in between and you are used to a partner doing things for you, it can be hard to be on your own, especially when you have nothing planned or things go wrong and the unexpected happens. This is where your friends come in. Good friends will support you when you need help, whether it's practical help or moral support. Good friends are in our lives for the long haul and will be there for us through thick and thin. They enrich our lives and remind us of how special and lovable we are. Friendships are what we rely on to help get us through and we must never, ever take them for granted. Friendships also enable us to keep giving, caring and sharing when we don't have an intimate partner. They help keep our hearts open and our spirits lifted. They care about how we're doing and are there when we need them. They are invaluable.

Enjoy your own company

Living a meaningful, fulfilled and independent life is a richly rewarding experience and it's something that we can develop and perfect. It requires willingness, curiosity, dedication, imagination, determination, awareness and skill. Even the relationship diehards among us can do it with enough desire and willpower. Anyone who wants to shine brightly and savour everything that life has to offer can practise the art. It's about listening to your own wisdom and having the strength to act on it and becoming more than you thought you were, more than you were told that you were. In the space in between you can reach into the deepest part of you and find the capacity to live life's contradictions and paradoxes, thrills and spills with good grace. If you can be alone and enjoy your own company you have given yourself the greatest gift. And the greatest gift to others is your own best self. It can be a liberating perspective to see that life can be a joy without a meaningful intimate relationship. Rather than going through life wondering if you'll meet your match soon or whether you'll eventually meet the right person, start living now and see your life as already fulfilling and meaningful.

 **brilliant** example

Let go of fears and find yourself

Margaret had always been in relationships but they had almost always been short-lived and had ended in disappointment. In our first coaching session, she explained to me that all she had ever wanted was to meet the right person and get married. At the time of our first meeting she was engaged and had become even more obsessed with getting married. But it became apparent in our conversation that she didn't really love her fiancé or have much in common with him. She had told herself that it was better to settle than risk not meeting someone with whom she was really compatible. Or worse – find herself alone. Over the coming weeks we focused on what made her feel alive and inspired about her own life and how she could develop herself as a person in her own right. Gradually, she came to face and let go of her fears of being alone and reconnected with her passion for learning languages and art. She and her fiancé parted company and she embraced the space in between and had time to find herself. She took up Italian and enjoyed wonderful trips to Italy. She had found a new joie de vivre.

Trust the process

Making the choice to enjoy the space in between and seeing it as a valuable experience is a wonderful testimony to your ability to live your own best life. All of our experiences shape us into the person we're becoming. Even if in your heart of hearts you know that you want to be in a relationship, until the right person comes along, enjoy the benefits of where you are right now. Trust that when you are ready for new love, you will find each other.

 **action**

Write down all the ways in which you are enjoying being on your own.

Is there one thing that you're learning by being on your own that you couldn't learn being part of a couple?

Which stage are you at?

Being single can happen at any stage in our lives and each one will carry its own challenges and rewards. In our twenties the possibilities are endless and we can apply our limitless energy towards becoming a self-assured and independent person. Most people are single at this stage and some will savour their freedom to play the field while others feel a strong pull to commit. If you're footloose and fancy free this is the time of self-discovery and a chance to explore passions and interests and get absorbed in what excites you. Meet as many people as you can – go on dates, take classes, join groups. The more life experiences you have, the better you'll know yourself. Use your drive and energy to explore options, meet people, make friends and try new things. The world's your oyster!

It's different for everyone, but as you progress through your twenties and into your thirties your biological clock might start ticking. If you're not part of a couple, it's easy to fall into the trap of thinking that time is running out and that everyone else is having babies except you. The challenge is to recognise that there are things in life which we can control and to make the most of those rather than focus on the things which we can't. There are always options and what's important is that you stay true to yourself and make decisions which are right for you and based on what you can do while letting go of the rest. This takes the stress and conflict out of your life and allows things to unfold in the best way possible.

> what's important is that you stay true to yourself and make decisions which are right for you

The mid-life crisis that we can hit in our forties means that some relationships become stale and fall apart. Whether you're single, divorced or widowed, when you get to your forties you ideally know yourself a lot better and are more comfortable in your own skin. At this stage you may feel inspired to change careers, start dating again or simply enjoy the freedom of going solo for a while. What's important is to be flexible and stay open to new experiences.

You have gained a lot of life experience and self-awareness by the time you reach your fifties and there's so much more living to do in the coming years and decades. The beauty of coming into mature adulthood is that you feel freer to be yourself and find what really engages you and you no longer worry about what people think. Hopefully, you trust yourself more and doubt yourself less. Life gives us many opportunities to realise our aspirations, pursue our interests and even heal past relationships. And there's no limit to when we can fall in love or discover something new about ourselves.

 **action**

Make a list of all the things that you are inspired to do with your life. Put the list somewhere where you can read it every day. Imagine where you'd like to go, what you'd like to see, what you'd like to learn, and what kind of people you'd like to meet. Really see yourself opening up to new experiences and feeling excited about what's coming your way. Be adventurous and try new things.

Overcome loneliness

Even when we truly enjoy our single lives, our spare time is filled with friends, family and social activities, we're taking the best care of ourselves and doing really well, from time to time we can still feel lonely. Sometimes our friends aren't available for a chat or we don't have anyone to spend the weekend with. Or we may be experiencing a deeper, more existential loneliness and longing. However we're feeling, when there's no one to cuddle up with in the middle of the night we can feel as if we're alone in the world, and wish we could find a special someone. In our darkest moments we might even question whether there is something wrong with us. Be prepared for these feelings by making a list of coping strategies and make sure that you do something that nurtures you on a deeper level and connects you with something meaningful to you. Strong feelings can often threaten to engulf us but if we allow them to wash over us and trust that we will still be intact, we develop more faith in our capacity to handle whatever comes up.

 **brilliant** action

Here are some strategies for overcoming feelings of loneliness:

● Practise deep breathing, positive affirmations and being kind and compassionate with yourself.

● Wrap yourself up in a cosy blanket, read an inspiring book or write to someone you love and trust.

● Go out for a lovely long walk. Keep moving until you feel your energy changing.

● Practise acceptance – open your arms wide and say 'yes' to life.

● If you're on your own on Valentine's Day, buy yourself expensive chocolates, flowers and celebrate you. Love and romance don't depend on anyone else.

Online dating

The space in between gives us time to think about whether we want to dip our toes in the water and start dating. Trust your intuition and know that you can change your mind at any moment. Some may wait for fate to take a hand while others may want to be more proactive. More and more people of all ages are signing up for internet dating sites and many strike lucky and meet their perfect match. There are so many dating sites so firstly you need to choose a site which appeals to you. You can often view people's profiles before paying for a subscription so explore different options, use your intuition and figure out which one is the best for you.

When you've decided on a dating site, you will need to write your profile. Some people can find it quite hard to write about themselves, especially the positive qualities. But unless you fully describe yourself, how is someone going to know that they are attracted to you? Decide four or five core adjectives that best describe you. If you find that hard to do, think about how your best friend would describe you. And then illustrate how you live that quality. For example, if you see yourself as an adventurer, say that you climbed the Himalayas or jumped out of a plane. Avoid clichés as they don't do anything to differentiate you. Lots of people are kind, warm and loving. Think about what is unique about you and makes you stand out. Paint a picture of yourself and be specific about the kind of person who you are looking to meet. Include some humour as this is a good way to establish rapport.

Be honest about who you are

In order to enhance your profile, choose a photo of you that you like and that is both natural and shows you at your best. You also need a stand out, positive headline. Those are the first two things that people see. Be honest in your description. Don't say that you love cooking when you'd much rather eat out. And unless you're prepared for the consequences, don't lie about your age. The main reason people do this is that they believe it will maximise their attraction. We can't make first impressions as we do in person, so we have to do the best we can with a photo and words. However, most people are concerned about honesty more than anything else, so think twice before editing your age.

Screen your responses

Seeing someone's photograph or reading their profile is very different from meeting them in person. For starters, you can't gauge if there's any chemistry and a photo can be deceiving. It's easy to find fault with people's profiles and make assumptions. So take everything into consideration rather than dissecting each piece of a person's profile and don't be so choosy that you price yourself out of the market. You may have fallen in love with someone in the past who wasn't your type, so don't dismiss people out of hand. By the same token, it's important to maintain your standards and not settle for someone who really doesn't match your criteria.

If you like the look of someone and they don't respond to you, you may be going for someone who isn't looking for someone like you. Very few people match our complete criteria so don't take it personally and stay open to different possibilities as long as they are a good match for you. Never compromise on the qualities that are most important to you (refer back to Chapter 1 'Get to know you'). If someone contacts you and you're not interested, you're not duty bound to respond. And if someone doesn't respond to you, don't see it as a rejection. If you want to give them the benefit of the doubt you can always wait a week and then send a short, polite message saying that you'd be interested in a dialogue with them. But only do this once.

When you first start communicating with a potential date, keep your emails brief and upbeat. Tell them why you answered their ad and what you like about their profile. If you keep it short, you'll have more to talk about next time. When you email, it's not always easy to feel a sense of connection and words can be misinterpreted, so at some point when trust and rapport have been established you'll progress to talking on the phone. Hearing someone's voice and actually speaking with them can tell you a lot more about them.

Going on a date

If you've struck up a conversation with someone, established that you like each other and enjoy talking to each other and you've progressed from sending messages to speaking on the phone, the next step will be meeting for a date. So what does a first date look like? There aren't any hard and fast answers.

 **brilliant** action

Close your eyes and think about your ideal first date. Do something that you'd really like but make your first date in the day and meet in a public place. You might want to have a boundary around how long you meet for. A great first date comes when there is a sense of trust and anticipation. You're not going on a blind date with a total stranger. You may not have met each other before but you've got to know each other on the phone. You like them, you're excited about them. You trust them. Never date someone who you've just emailed once.

What if you don't feel chemistry on the first date? Don't throw the baby out with the bath water if your heart isn't pounding on first meeting. Someone may not look like a film star but they might be warm, funny, intelligent and caring. Be open to someone who isn't necessarily your type. It's more important to date someone who makes you feel good about yourself.

Sometimes dates don't work out for whatever reason. If that happens, just move on. You may have to kiss a few frogs, but if you do click with someone you will want to have a few dates with them to really establish whether you are both interested in having a committed relationship with each other. You'll then want to remove your profiles and embark on what hopefully becomes a wonderfully happy relationship.

A more rounded you

The space in between is an important rite of passage to a fuller and more rounded version of ourselves. In this space you can learn to value yourself more and be empowered by making your own decisions. Ultimately, you may want to share your life with someone special but you have found a way of really enjoying your own company and being happy on your own. When you accept yourself, you are relaxed about finding the right partner because you know how to be happy. You recognise the value of finding your raison d'être and pursuing your dreams. When you feel flat or suffer a setback – which will inevitably happen – you find strength and abilities that you might not have developed in a relationship. There will be times when the grass is greener and you long for that special someone. The irony is that people who are in a relationship sometimes wish for the autonomy that comes with forging your own path. There are benefits to both. Wherever you are, make the most of it and trust that this is exactly where you are meant to be.

 brilliant recap

The space in between gives you an opportunity to give more to yourself and develop a deeper sense of being a person in your own right. There are endless possibilities and life choices at this stage of life if you are willing to embrace being alone and discover the joys of living – and loving – life to the full. You will bring even more to an intimate relationship when the time is right.

 brilliant task for the week

Keep focusing on all the choices that you have in the space in between and commit to becoming a more whole, happy and fulfilled you. Do one thing every day which celebrates your time to yourself.

CHAPTER 6

Transform your relationship patterns

When you struggle with your partner, you are struggling with yourself. Every fault you see in them touches a denied weakness in yourself.

Deepak Chopra, doctor,
best-selling author and public speaker

Our intimate relationships offer us enormous potential for personal growth and happiness. We discover so much about ourselves in relationships, and although much of this discovery is joyful and exciting, it can also be hugely challenging. Falling in love can put us in touch with emotional patterns that need to be healed and help us to see the false beliefs and unhealthy behaviours that we've adopted and which need to be changed. You don't have to be perfect to have a relationship. If that were so, none of us would have one. But, as you go into a relationship, allow yourself to be open to the need for healing and how your partner can help. A relationship reveals not only all that needs to be healed, but with willingness and co-operation, it provides support and the means for healing to take place. It takes commitment to get past the romance stage and deepen your relationship and there are many stages and steps along the way. Each time you move through a new challenge, you will heal more of the fear, conflicts, sacrifices, feelings of unworthiness, guilt and old self-defeating patterns.

We don't necessarily go into relationships expecting to be challenged. In fact, we are more likely to be resistant to the idea, at least initially, of taking a long hard look at ourselves and our patterns. That's usually because we know or intuit that the journey of growing self-awareness can be somewhat of a bumpy ride. Just think about it – who brings out the most intense feelings and reactions in you as much as an intimate partner? Who challenges you to develop emotionally and affects you in ways that nobody else does? Our intimate relationships reach the parts that others cannot reach. They get through our defences and penetrate the core of our vulnerability. They activate our fears and longings. They also connect us with our unresolved issues and the aspects of ourselves that we try to hide – our shadow side – more than anything else. Even though this can be a painful process it can, paradoxically, open us up to the greatest joy – that of being in a totally authentic and fulfilling relationship.

Relationships are a mirror

How does this happen? Basically, your partner acts like a mirror, reflecting back to you everything about yourself – both the positive and the negative. When we are blinded by love, we tend to only see the positive. We are attracted to people whose qualities and characteristics we admire or aspire towards. It's as if we are falling in love with ourselves. This creates a feeling of compatibility, harmony and validation and a sense that we've made the right choice. As the relationship evolves, however, we inevitably begin to see traits and behaviours in our partners that we don't identify with and don't like. At first we may try to gloss over these, as they make us feel uncomfortable. But in the same way as the irritating presence of a grain of sand in an oyster creates a pearl, bearing the discomfort of our own reac-

> your partner acts like a mirror, reflecting back to you everything about yourself

tion and finding out what it says about us can be illuminating. The self-awareness we glean offers us the key to being in the best relationship with both ourselves and our intimate partners.

Why do we repeat negative patterns?

Have you ever found yourself repeating a negative pattern in your relationships? Consciously you may want to break these patterns, but somehow they still keep recurring. Typical scenarios include getting involved with the same kind of people and recreating the same kind of painful experiences, or getting stuck in a vicious cycle with your partner and not knowing how to get out of it. So why exactly do we keep repeating patterns that undermine our ability to be happy and create loving relationships? And how can we change these recurring patterns? To answer these questions, we need to take a deeper look at our own psychology.

We are multifaceted by nature and each of us contains a wide spectrum of personality traits, innate characteristics and potential behaviours. Some of them we are aware of and some we are not. Some of these are encouraged and praised by our parents, other authority figures and society at large, such as being kind, thoughtful, polite, hard working and law abiding. Others are deemed bad or negative and are actively discouraged or even condemned. These include such feelings as rage, jealousy, shame, resentment, lust, greed and all the aggressive and sexual tendencies we consider forbidden, dangerous or, in extreme cases, evil.

Because these aspects of human nature are deemed reprehensible and we feel uncomfortable accepting them in ourselves, they become part of our 'dark side'. When this happens, a shadow personality is created within us. This hidden part of us contains all our repressed aspects which we deny expression. However, just because we banish these rejected facets of ourselves it doesn't mean that they cease to exist. Instead, they form the part of us that we hide away – not only from others but also ourselves. More often than not, the feelings, traits and qualities that we pretend don't belong to us are the ones we consider to be negative.

Many of us find it hard to accept our negative traits because we believe that we need to be perfect to be loved. We fear that if our partners knew what we were really like, they would reject us. So we don't confront what we are afraid of in ourselves and we attempt to keep secrets from ourselves in the hope that we can avoid dealing with our shadow side. We often deny our anger, selfishness and unacceptable behaviours, as well as our other negative qualities, to avoid confronting our limitations or showing our vulnerability. Instead, we create a façade that masks our true selves. The truth is that none of us is perfect and the only way we can be loved and accepted by others is to embrace all of who we are – warts and all. But first we need to discover our unlived parts. And it's our intimate relationships which offer us the best clues.

> many of us believe that we need to be perfect to be loved

brilliant tip

We project what we don't like or recognise about ourselves on to others. As we become aware of our hidden traits and qualities, we can begin to create conscious, authentic and fulfilling relationships.

Become aware of what you hide

All of us have parts of ourselves that we have denied or disowned. So how do we become conscious of our hidden side?

The answer is through becoming aware of something that we all do – it's called 'projection'. Just as in the same way that a movie camera projects an image on to a screen, we unconsciously project on to others all those aspects of ourselves that we don't want to acknowledge and that we are afraid of, embarrassed about or ashamed of. In fact, any facet of ourselves that we cut off from – positive or negative – we will tend to perceive as belonging to others. How does this work in practice? Try this test.

 **action**

Start by thinking about your partner's irritating traits, especially the ones that really get on your nerves. If you're not in a relationship, think about the traits that most annoyed you about your previous partner and write them down.

The qualities that most annoy me about my partner are:

1

2

3

4

5

6

From your list, are there any characteristics that you have a particularly strong reaction to? Believe it or not, it's almost certainly because you share those same traits but you just haven't admitted it to yourself. For example, you may fear your partner's anger, not realising that it is your own capacity for anger that you fear.

Now list all the traits you do not like in other people – for instance, vanity, selfishness, anger, arrogance, bad manners, unreliability, greed, etc. Come

▶

up with as many as you can and keep adding to your list. You might be surprised at how many there are! Are there any that you have to admit you recognise in yourself? Even if you don't think that any of them belong to you, are you open to the possibility that they just might?

Understand your reactions

Of course, not all our criticisms of others are projections of our own undesirable traits. Sometimes the way in which we react to others is based on our core values and our moral and ethical code. The way to know the difference is *how* you respond. If you overreact or get excessively emotional, it's likely that something unconscious in you is being activated. For example, if your partner is arrogant, it is completely reasonable for you to find this unacceptable. But if your reaction is unduly excessive, you can be sure that you are unwittingly projecting on to your partner the very same trait that you aren't fully aware of or don't like about yourself.

 action

The next time you get into an argument with your partner or find yourself reacting strongly to one of their traits or behaviours, stop for a moment and take a look at yourself. And ask yourself the following questions:

● What part of me is like this person?

● Have I met this trait before in a previous partner?

● How can I use my reaction to learn something about myself?

● In what way would my relationship benefit from me becoming more aware of myself?

It takes courage to look at ourselves in this way but unless we do we will keep repeating negative patterns ad infinitum. Recognising what belongs to us and integrating our unlived parts means we can create a new template for honest and authentic relationships.

brilliant example

Move from a self-defeating pattern to a self-empowering one

Kim and Luke had been together for a couple of years when I first met them. They both admitted that their relationship was failing and that they were making each other miserable. On talking with them, it became apparent that they were stuck in old patterns and that they were negatively projecting on to each other.

Kim had never really opened up to Luke and revealed her vulnerable side and as a way of protecting herself from hurt, she often got angry with what she perceived as Luke's lack of warmth and commitment.

Luke on the other hand experienced Kim as aggressive and unfeeling and often kept his distance. So they reinforced their perceptions of each other and perpetuated their unhappiness. As we began to explore their patterns, Kim and Luke began to become more conscious of how they were behaving and why and the way in which their behaviour was impacting on their relationship. Slowly they each began to take responsibility for healing their past hurts and disappointments and this meant that they were able to relate differently to each other and appreciate each other's positive qualities. Their relationship has blossomed ever since and they now enjoy a happy and fulfilling relationship.

It's not just our perceived negative traits that we tend to deny and relegate to the unconscious – we disown our positive qualities as well. Why is that? Usually it's because we simply don't have the confidence to express everything that is wonderful about us. When we don't acknowledge what is good about us, we stay small and don't take responsibility for and develop our unique talents, gifts and positive attributes. And we either end up admiring others and wishing we could be like them in some way, or feeling envy or resentment towards them. Neither of these enables us or our relationships to flourish. In fact we are more likely to sabotage our relationships when we don't own up to the truth of who we are. The more you 'own' your positive qualities and give yourself credit for them, the more rooted you will be in your true self. And the more able you will be to find expression for everything that is wonderful about you.

 **brilliant** action

Take some time to think about all the qualities that you admire or envy in either your current or a previous partner and write them down.

The qualities that I admire or envy in others are:

1

2

3

4

5

Once you've compiled your list, begin to reflect on how many of these qualities actually belong to you. Some may be easier to recognise than others. Some you may not relate to at all, but that doesn't mean that you don't possess them. It may simply mean that they have lain dormant. When you've had time to consider the qualities you've listed, ask yourself the following questions:

● What would happen if I expressed the qualities on my list?

● How would I feel about myself?

- How would my partner feel about me?
- What impact might this have on my relationship?
- How would my relationship change?

What we do not know can and does hurt us and others too

The template for our relationship patterns is created to a large extent by our family of origin. As infants and children we are totally dependent on our parents or caretakers for our physical survival. Not only that, but our ability to grow emotionally and thrive depends on how loved and nurtured we were and how able our parents were to prepare and equip us for independence and adulthood. How successfully this challenge was met will have a huge influence on our psychological make-up. However, no matter how well-intentioned our parents were, many of us will have experienced some kind of wounding in our relationship with them.

It's not uncommon to feel disappointed, let down, betrayed or angry with our parents for not meeting our demands and expectations. The intensity of these feelings will partly depend on our temperament but largely depend on our family dynamic. For example, if one or both of your parents was dominant, controlling or authoritarian, you will have almost certainly experienced a sense of powerlessness. If this feeling continues into adulthood, you may well 'choose' (this is invariably an unconscious choice) a controlling partner who fits your template, and so perpetuate the feeling of powerlessness. Or, you might adopt another strategy and 'choose' a partner who is weak, so that you get to feel strong and powerful in contrast. However, this isn't an

> we keep being drawn to people with whom we can re-enact our early patterning

authentic strength, as it is dependent on someone else being weak. As long as the legacy of our early conditioning remains unconscious, we will keep being drawn to people with whom we can re-enact our early patterning. These people will in turn be attracted to you because you will mirror each other in some way. This sets up a very painful dynamic in which both parties suffer and remain stuck.

Healing our patterns

But there is a positive side to this. We often repeat a pattern in our relationships until we become more conscious of it and ultimately heal it. This is what psychologists call 'repetition compulsion'. For example, if you tend to get involved with people who dominate and control you and you don't recognise this pattern or attempt to change it, you will almost certainly attract the same kind of dynamic in the next relationship. This sets up a painful vicious cycle which can only be broken when you become aware of this recurring pattern and why you are recreating the same scenario.

None of us consciously sets out to experience the same hurt that we felt in a previous relationship. We wouldn't be that masochistic. It is often bewildering, frustrating, upsetting and demoralising to find ourselves repeating a negative pattern, especially when we are at a loss as to why we keep tripping ourselves up in this way. Carl Jung said that the psyche is always striving for wholeness, and one of the ways in which this happens is by attracting partners into our lives who can help us to integrate the disowned parts of ourselves. In that sense, everyone is our teacher, whether they are aware of it or not. Some lessons we grasp very easily and others take longer to learn. Some are relatively pain-free, while others can connect us to our deepest wounds.

 **action**

Make a list of your past relationships. You may have a short or long list, several short relationships or just one long one. This exercise may trigger different feelings in you, some painful, some sad, some happy and sweet. Take your time and be gentle with yourself as you reflect on your previous relationships and don't judge yourself or your partner.

Look at these relationships objectively and acknowledge what wasn't working in each of these relationships and why they didn't last. Focus on any fears, insecurities and emotions that you experienced and the part that they played in the quality and outcome of your relationships. Look at the common denominators in these relationships. Have you attracted similar experiences? Is there a recurring theme and, if so, what is it? What does this reveal about you?

As you start to become aware of your patterns you will begin to see yourself more clearly. This is a very empowering process and will enable you to create new, healthy patterns based on who you really are. Your authenticity will give you the freedom to enjoy close, honest and loving relationships. And experience the joy of being totally yourself and loved for who you are.

From fantasy to reality

However much we think we know why we are attracted to certain people, our rationale is only the tip of the iceberg. Apart from our deeper agenda of wanting to become aware of and heal our patterns, there is another factor that influences our relationship choices. We each carry an inner image of the kind of partner we are seeking. Our parents and our intrinsic nature shape such images. However, what happens is that we frequently and unknowingly paint these inner images on to people we are attracted to, and we believe that that is who they really are. In the same way as we project our disowned selves on to our partners, we will also project this inner image of our ideal partner on to whoever is a good 'hook'. However, given the nature of projection, the qualities and characteristics we 'see' in others don't always exist in reality.

For example, your inner image of your ideal partner might be of someone strong, powerful and heroic, or selfless, compassionate and unconditionally loving. Whatever your inner image is, you will be attracted to people who appear to embody those qualities. Sometimes the person we fall in love with matches our inner image – at least at the beginning. But often we are disappointed when our ideal and the reality of the person don't quite match up. Consider this – how many times have you got involved with someone and 'seen' them in a particular way, only to find out that they weren't what you thought they were at all? How did you feel? Let down, cheated, misled, betrayed, angry or disappointed? Did you believe that it was your partner who had changed? Although some people do consciously deceive their partners into thinking they are something they're not, mostly we deceive ourselves. When our image of our partners clashes with reality, it's as if a spell is broken. And we wake up to the truth of who we are in a relationship with.

> often we are disappointed when our ideal and the reality of the person don't quite match up

This awakening – however rude – also offers us a glimpse into our own nature. When you see your partner as a mere mortal, you have a choice. You can either blame or resent them for not conforming to your idealised image. Or you can begin to see them for who they are – a complex mix of different qualities and flaws, strengths and weaknesses – just like you. And you can make the more challenging choice of seeing the part you have played in this story. This enables your relationship to become more rooted in awareness and reality.

 **action**

Think about what type of person you are attracted to.

- What do they look like?
- What is it about these people that fascinates and enthrals you?
- How do they make you feel when you are with them?
- What might this say about the inner image you carry of your ideal partner?
- How often have you fallen in love with an image only to wake up to a very different reality? Describe what happened.

Give yourself time to think about these questions. Becoming aware of the kind of person you feel irresistibly drawn to and understanding why this person feels so compelling to you takes time. But it's a fascinating journey and what you discover about yourself in the process empowers you to create more conscious and committed relationships.

 **recap**

It's what we don't know about ourselves that tends to hurt us. We often blithely go into relationships without knowing who we really are or who the other person really is. When we have a better understanding of our own psychology and become aware of our relationship patterns then we can choose more positive, affirming ways of being in a relationship.

brilliant task for the week

Choose one recurring relationship pattern and see whether it is still operative in your life. Commit to changing it and becoming more mindful of how this pattern plays out. If you are in a relationship, talk to your partner about a relationship pattern and see how open and receptive they are to what you have to say.

CHAPTER 7

Choose your perfect match

Love alone can unite living beings so as to complete and fulfil them ... for it alone joins them by what is deepest in themselves.

Pierre Teilhard de Chardin,
theologian and philosopher

At some point in our lives we all embark on the quest to find someone to love and who will love us in return. Sometimes we hit lucky straight away. At other times we think we've found the right person and feel ecstatically happy for a while, only to feel let down or deceived further down the line. Our lovers weren't who we thought they were and didn't match up to our expectations. Although these experiences may seem inevitable to most of us, we actually have a lot more control over the kind of relationships we attract than we realise. So much of the painful trial-and-error process involved in finding the right partner can be alleviated if we take the time to know what we really want.

It's important to have a clear idea in your mind of who you want to be with before you put energy into finding someone. Only you will know what type of person you really connect with – no one else can dictate that to you. We have all had the experience of meeting someone we thought would make us happy and then finding out that they weren't really right for us at all. We can avoid this hit-and-miss approach by following a few easy steps.

Trust your intuition

Have you ever failed to follow your intuition or repressed your instincts about somebody only to realise later that you should have paid more attention? One of your best allies in knowing if you are making the right choices is your own inner knowing. Just think about it. The moment you meet someone, there is usually a voice within that tells you if that person is someone you can trust, connect and feel safe with. So why don't we always listen to it? Well, when it comes to romantic love, sexual chemistry and our emotions are usually much louder and more urgent and may drown out our inner voice. But if you are serious about finding your perfect match, it's imperative that you listen to the messages that your inner voice is telling you. No matter how out of practice you are at tuning into and following your inner knowing, your intuition will always guide you in the right direction if you listen to it.

> your intuition will always guide you in the right direction if you listen to it

Learning to listen to your inner compass is essential to attracting what will fulfil and nurture you on all levels. So what is that inner knowing? People experience it in different ways, but you could say first and foremost that it is a feeling. Your feelings about someone – any insights you have, intuition, deep certainties – are messages from your inner knowing. They come before you have time to rationalise. Inner knowing is simply a gut feeling.

brilliant action

Have you ever got involved with someone even though your intuition was telling you not to?

● Did your gut feeling prove right after all?

● What happened?

- What did you learn from this experience?
- Did you resolve to follow your instincts the next time?

Has there ever been a time when you did go with your gut feeling and not get into a relationship with someone, even though you felt attracted to them on some level?

- What made you trust your inner knowing?
- Has this enabled you to feel more confident in your own ability to make the right choices for you?
- Has your intuition become part of the litmus test when assessing your compatibility with someone?

What influences your choices?

How do you go about meeting your perfect match? Whether you prefer to be proactive or leave it to fate, you first need to feel confident that you can trust in your ability to make good choices. Finding the right person requires that you know yourself well enough to know what's best for you and what kind of person you would be happy and fulfilled with. It's also important to recognise how ready you are for a relationship and how you really feel about getting intimately involved with someone.

When you are considering what kind of relationship you would like to be in, it's worth asking yourself whether your desire for a relationship is motivated by the need to feel complete or to find someone to complement you. If it's the former, you may be looking for someone who makes up for what you perceive as a deficit in you. We often seek out people who will fill a need or emptiness in us, and this can lead to an unhealthy dependency in which neither person is able to grow. For example, if you are looking for someone financially successful, it may be because *you* feel insecure in that area. You are far more likely to attract the qualities that you want in a partner when you feel a sense of wholeness rather than a lack. Becoming aware of what under-pins your criteria in choosing a partner gives you the best chance of making a healthy and conscious choice.

 **tip**

When you feel whole, you attract the same quality in another person.

Enhance your ability to attract a partner

 **action**

Take a look at the list below and see how many statements ring true for you.

- I want but don't need to be in a relationship.
- I live in harmony with my needs and values.
- I have healthy self-esteem and I know my worth.
- I keep my life in balance.
- I have a good circle of friends.
- I enjoy my work.
- I see romance and sex as part of a relationship, not the whole relationship.
- I am realistic about the kind of relationship I want.
- I am confident that I will choose someone who is the best for me.

If you agreed with all or most of these statements it's highly likely that you are happy with yourself and your life, and attracting your perfect match would simply serve to double your happiness.

Being happy with yourself makes you much more magnetic to others. In fact, often we attract the best partners when we are neither looking for nor avoiding the possibility of finding someone. Living your life to the full while being completely open to meeting someone is a powerful combination. After all, the key to your happiness

> live your best life and you will attract your best partner

and the quality of your relationships ultimately depend on your ability to be comfortable and content with who you are. When you acknowledge and appreciate your inherent worth, you invite others to do the same. In other words, live your best life and you will attract your best partner.

What are your criteria?

Creating a checklist of what you do and do not want in a relationship helps you to determine what's really important to you in a partner. The qualities that you seek in a relationship need to reflect your core values. For example, on a very pragmatic level, if health and fitness are of primary importance to you, it is entirely reasonable for you to want your partner to be a non-smoker. This might be called one of your 'non-negotiable' criteria. It's important that you hold fast to what you know you definitely do and don't want in a partner. There is no right or wrong here and your list will be unique to you. Don't be swayed by what others consider important. Be true to your own criteria and values and don't settle for less. Of course there will be areas in which you will need to be more flexible, as some compromise is required in any relationship. Being overly rigid about things like hair colour or the car a person drives might be limiting your options somewhat! But to give your relationship the best chance of success, you need to hold out for the qualities that feel like essential requirements.

Be specific

When you're vague about what you want in a partner, you're leaving a lot to chance and risking your own happiness. In fact, to deny even one important quality is denying an essential part of who you are and compromises your integrity. It gives out the message that you're willing to settle for someone who falls short in some way. To draw the right person to you, it is absolutely essential that you know where you stand and become aware of what you want.

If you've already thought about what you want in a partner and created your 'wish list', see this process as an opportunity to re-evaluate your criteria. You might discover that you have listed some new qualities that you hadn't considered important before. Sometimes we can feel resistance to being specific about what we want. Writing your list connects you with your deep desire for a partner and this can bring up feelings of vulnerability. Sometimes our desire to be in a relationship brings up feelings of sadness or regret from the past. And focusing on what we want can seem like a painful reminder of what we long for or miss. This isn't necessarily negative, however. Your longing can galvanise you and connect you with your capacity to love. Allow yourself to feel whatever comes up as you compose your list of qualities, and see this as a powerful way of connecting you with your heart's desire.

brilliant action

Write a list of qualities in a partner that you have ever desired, dreamt about or contemplated. Don't limit yourself – put down every characteristic that you can think of (more than 10 if necessary). This will help you to get clear about what you are looking for in a partner.

1

2

3

4

5

6

7

8

9

10

Choose your top 10 from your list and place them in order of priority. Now take a look at each one in turn. For example, if 'successful' is one of your qualities, ask yourself what that might look like in reality. For example, what would someone need to have achieved in order for you to identify them as successful? How much money would they need to have? What kind of lifestyle do you envisage them leading? Challenge your assumptions and explore more deeply what you mean by such qualities as attractive or reliable. What is the underlying characteristic of each quality? For example, if 'supportive' is one of your top qualities, what is it about being supportive that you value and are attracted to in someone? This might seem obvious at first. But it's only when we dig a little deeper and ask ourselves some probing questions that we can determine why the qualities we are looking for are so important to us.

If you're uncertain whether you should be steadfast or flexible about a particular quality that's important to you, ask yourself the following question: 'Would this quality support who and what I am?' If the answer is yes, then you know it's an essential requirement that you can't compromise.

Make sure that you can be quiet and not interrupted for a few minutes. Close your eyes and focus on your breathing for a moment. When you are feeling still and centred, imagine being in a relationship with someone supportive and allow the feeling of their support to fill your being. How does it feel? Perhaps you are experiencing a feeling of safety, of being ▶

accepted and validated. Or maybe the support of your partner gives you the confidence to shine more fully and be more of who you are. Ask yourself whether you have felt this way in other relationships.

Being supported may be something you have come to expect, or there may be a wound associated with this particular quality for you. The more you deepen your understanding of what you want and why it is so important to you, the more clearly you are able to attract a partner who embodies the qualities you are seeking. And when you clearly define the type of person you want, you're much more likely to recognise that person when you meet them. As you define and refine your relationship list, you are increasing your chances of meeting someone with whom you share a strong affinity.

 **tip**

In order to attract a partner who embodies your core values and desires, you need to be clear and articulate what you want.

Your reality check

Defining your top 10 traits not only clarifies what you most value, it also illuminates your own qualities. Being specific is your way of taking a reality check and making sure that you're not looking for qualities that don't match who you are. While it is true that each person brings different qualities to a relationship, it is also true that people tend to gravitate towards others who already possess the qualities they value. For example, if one of the qualities you seek in someone is commitment, you need to know that you are able to match that quality and make the kind of commitment that you expect of a partner.

 **example**

Know what you want in a partner

Katie had never really given much thought to what was really important to her in a partner. She had been in quite a few relationships and felt that she had got into them more by accident than by design. She invariably ended up feeling emotionally drained by her partners, and the relationships had always ended messily. Katie spent a long time compiling her list of qualities and then I suggested that we clarify some of them so that she could understand their importance to her more fully. One of her top 10 qualities was 'independent'. I asked her what that meant to her and whether it involved being with someone who had their own interests or who had no desire to tie her down. After a deeper exploration and much discussion of what being independent meant to Katie, it became apparent that she wanted to be with someone who wasn't emotionally needy and who could take care of themselves. She then added self-reliant, resourceful and emotionally mature to the list, as she felt that these were qualities that she had worked hard to develop in herself and valued very highly. After clarifying all her qualities, Katie felt that next time she met someone she felt attracted to, she would have a much clearer sense of whether that person was right for her or not.

The magic of synchronicity

Finding a partner doesn't entirely depend on our efforts. Carl Jung described synchronicity as a meaningful coincidence in which our inner and outer realities coincide. In other words, when you and your future partner are ready for a new relationship, something will conspire to put you in the right place at the right time to meet that person. It's as if the destiny of each person is fulfilled by that seemingly chance meeting, and there is often a feeling of rightness and inevitability about such a union. So although we do have free will in how we go into a relationship, we also need to trust that the timing and circumstances of how we meet someone will be perfect. That doesn't mean that we have to leave everything to chance or passively wait for someone to show up in our lives. When you are ready for a relationship you might want to take a much more proactive role in meeting someone and let the world know that you are available. How you do that will be your choice, but transmitting your desire for a relationship – whether it be joining an internet dating site or declaring it to the Universe – will increase your chances of attracting someone into your orbit.

How to know whether you've found your match

Imagine that you've just met someone you really like. You've prepared yourself for a relationship by taking the best care of you, and you've been working on changing any negative patterns. You know who and what you want and your inner knowing is giving you the green light about this person. The next step is to discover whether they possess the qualities that you are seeking in a partner. Some traits, like how attractive they are to you and their sense of humour, are apparent. And others, such as their taste in food or music, are easy to talk about. But many qualities take longer to uncover. How, for example, can you tell if someone is honest or reliable, without putting them on the spot?

One effective way of discovering whether someone matches the qualities you are seeking is to decide which one you are most curious about and share a story or experience that you have that highlights it. For example, if honesty is one of your top qualities, you might talk about a situation in which someone acted dishonestly and the consequences of that deception. Listen carefully to the response that your story gets before you discuss your own feelings. Does the other person approve of such behaviour or are they more tolerant of dishonesty? You might also share a situation in which you weren't completely honest and see whether they are able to empathise or admit to a similar scenario themselves. This will help you to gauge where they stand on this important quality. Other qualities, such as respectful and considerate, will reveal themselves in people's actions. If you notice that a prospective partner treats people with respect and consideration it's likely that they will behave in the same way towards you.

Make mental notes when you first meet someone and remain alert and observant. What people tell you about themselves when you first meet them can be very revealing – sometimes strikingly so. A client of mine asked her date whether he was available, and he answered 'I am and I'm not'. Although she went ahead with the relationship, it ultimately ended as

> what people tell you about themselves when you first meet them can be very revealing

he wasn't able to make a commitment to her. At other times the messages are more subtle and take time to decipher.

Share your passions

Although good relationships need contrast as well as similarities, it's important to know what you have in common. Discussing your likes and dislikes and sharing your passions in life will give you an immediate sense of whether someone has any interest in the things that turn you on. Your passions say a lot about who you are, and what inspires and motivates you. Find out about each other's hopes and dreams and how excited you feel about them. Your ability to resonate with what makes each of you feel alive is a good indicator of how vibrant and supportive your relationship will feel.

Take your time

It takes time to get to know whether someone is right for you. Going slowly and not rushing into a relationship gives you the benefit of discovering whether you are making the right choice for you. Falling in love at first sight or becoming instantly infatuated might feel intoxicating, but getting involved too quickly means that you have very little to go on, other than the feelings that are sweeping you away. You need time to get to know the other person and time for them to know you. That way you can establish whether a potential relationship between you is based on complementary personalities. You owe it to yourself to take the time to get to know someone before embarking on a romantic relationship. Why risk a broken heart just because you didn't take the time to get to know who you were getting involved with?

No matter how familiar someone seems to you or how connected you feel to them, it's important to remember that they are in fact a total stranger to you. A sense of déjà vu with this person can simply mean that they remind you of someone or that you are repeating a pattern and not that you are necessarily destined to be together. Don't let the fact that you feel a strong connection with someone you hardly know blind you to finding out more about them. The more you know about a person, the more potential problems you can rule out. For example, if you have had a pattern of getting involved with people who are afraid of commitment, it would be wise to ask about a prospective partner's track record and the reason for the break-up of their past relationships. You can do this without it being an interrogation – simply make it clear that you are interested in getting to know them.

> the more you know about a person, the more potential problems you can rule out

We all have an ideal self that we initially present to others in order to impress them, and it takes time to drop our façades and show all of who we are. And just because you like someone and feel attracted to them doesn't mean that you are right for each other. When you take time to get to know someone you can observe them in different situations and moods, and find out whether their values and attitudes are compatible with yours and how comfortable you are with each other. This will give you a real indication of how lasting and happy any relationship is likely to be.

 brilliant recap

Knowing what you want in a partner helps you to make a more informed and conscious choice in your relationships. First impressions can be deceiving and it's important to listen to your inner knowing about whether someone is right for you. Taking it slowly and getting to know someone before you become intimately involved gives you the best chance of creating a successful relationship.

 brilliant task for the week

Spend some more time contemplating your list of qualities. If you're in a relationship, do you feel that your partner embodies them? If you're single, how many of your top qualities belong to ex-partners? Have you added any qualities to the list since your last relationship?

CHAPTER 8

Enjoy balance and harmony in your relationships

Peace of mind comes from not wanting to change others, but by simply accepting them as they are. True acceptance is always without demands and expectations.

Gerald Jampolsky, author and psychiatrist

Have you ever found yourself struggling to reconcile the differences between you and your partner? Maybe you have secretly thought that if only you were more like your partner or that they were more like you, your relationship, would work better. Our differences can add spice to our relationships but they can also create conflict and feel intimidating or even threatening. When we accept each other as we are, we feel enriched by our differences and our relationships thrive. But when we perceive ourselves as better or worse than our partners, our relationships fail to grow. Overvaluing or devaluing ourselves doesn't allow us to be truly intimate or to create a sense of equality in our relationships. In fact, seeing ourselves as above or below our partners is more likely to create a sense of competition, and distance us from each other.

However similar or dissimilar you and your partner are, the reality is that no two people are completely alike. Our parents, upbringing, innate character and life experiences shape and define our uniqueness. Each of us will have our own patterning and express our different strengths and weaknesses and approaches to life in our own individual way. Some of us are innately confident, bold and adventurous and have no problem taking the initiative or making decisions, and others are more hesitant or timid when it comes to taking a risk or being proactive. Sometimes our differences complement each other – one partner's spontaneous or impulsive side might be tempered by the other's more considered and measured approach. At other times our different temperaments, characteristics and approaches can cause tension and disagreement. The good news is that no matter how much we vary in character and attitude and how challenging this can feel, if we are willing to value and accept our differences then we can create a sense of equality in our relationships.

 **brilliant** tip

When we accept and respect each other, we feel loved and appreciated, and this creates a sense of equality in our relationships.

What is an equal relationship?

An equal relationship is one in which each person is seen as equal in the other's eyes. This creates a healthy and mutually respectful dynamic in which each person feels validated and authentic. An equal relationship doesn't mean that two people have to match each other in everything, or that they are equal in all respects. Couples will naturally have different abilities, attitudes, strengths and weaknesses and areas of expertise. But in an equal relationship these balance each other out and each person feels whole and in their own right in the relationship and is treated as such. For example, your partner may have a more highly paid job than you. But that may be balanced by the fact that you have a very wide circle of wonderful friends. The fact that your partner's life is enriched by you in this way creates a point of balance and equality. Achieving equality in our relationships is rarely a given and often requires a conscious effort. However, until we become more aware of ourselves, our expectations

> achieving equality in our relationships is rarely a given and often requires a conscious effort

and our patterns, we can unwittingly create and get stuck in unequal dynamics in our relationships. When this happens, we don't feel good about ourselves or our relationship.

Why is equality so important?

Equality is a crucial factor in successful relationships. Where there is equality, there is mutual respect, acceptance and consideration, and each person feels loved and appreciated. Where there is inequality, there are likely to be power struggles and sacrifice. For example, in some relationships one partner – usually unconsciously – might elect to play the 'parent' while the other person takes on the role of the 'child'. In this scenario the 'parent' has all the power and control and the 'child' is disempowered and dependent. The 'parent' will take control and make all the decisions and the 'child' will acquiesce and submit to the 'parent's' wishes. In this kind of dynamic both people need the other to maintain their respective roles. As long as the status quo is maintained, the 'parent' stays in control and never has to face their insecurities and vulnerabilities, and the 'child' remains dependent and never has to grow up and take responsibility for themselves. The result is that both people remain stuck, and sacrifice their chances of growth and happiness. This can create huge resentment, anger or even rage, in which one or both parties blames the other for their unhappy relationship. Although this example is at the extreme end of the spectrum, many relationships contain shades of this kind of inequality.

Recognising codependency

Do you feel a constant need for certainty in your relationship? Are you always looking for reassurance from your partner because you're fearful about it not working out? If that is the case, you may be codependent. Codependency initially described a person who was in a relationship with someone with an addiction. However, over time it has come to describe anyone who has a dependency on a specific relationship. If you are codependent, you will derive your identity from your relationship. But, far from this making you happy, you are much more likely to feel deeply insecure within the relationship and be driven by a desperate need to maintain it. This leads to very controlling behaviour, such as the continual monitoring of such things as your partner's plans, social activities and even their feelings. The constant worry and stress of being codependent is exacerbated by obsessive analysing of the relationship. All of which can contribute to a feeling of being completely out of balance. If you recognise any of these signs, reread Chapters 1, 2 and 5 and commit to spending some time by yourself, reassessing your values and getting to know and appreciate yourself better.

Don't go changing

Have you ever adjusted your priorities or discounted your preferences in order to please your partner? It may be something as simple and seemingly innocuous as the way you dress, your diet or how much time you spend with your friends. Of course we naturally make some adjustments when we are in a relationship, because there are two people's needs to consider. But if your desire to please your partner is at the expense of who you are and what you really want and need, then you are basically making your partner more important than you and putting your relationship on a very unequal footing. More importantly, you are devaluing yourself and creating a serious dent in your self-esteem. Always respect your wants and needs and never tell yourself that they aren't important. Being true to yourself is the greatest gift you can give yourself *and* others, and a relationship in which both people are honouring themselves and each other has the greatest chance of success.

> ### brilliant tip
>
> Never change anything about yourself in order to please your partner. Being true to yourself is the best way of honouring yourself and your relationship.

Redress the balance

When you first meet someone it's exciting, and you can't help but focus much of your energy on the new relationship. Falling in love is intoxicating and can feel all-consuming. In the early heady days of love we never stop talking and delight in sharing our thoughts and opinions on everything. But the kind of exclusive attention that you give to a new relationship can be a dangerous precedent to set. Even at the beginning of a relationship it's important to have time for yourself, to cultivate your own life and preserve your identity. So how much energy and attention do you and your partner give to your relationship? It would be unrealistic to expect that the energy, attention, effort and interest in your relationship is equally expressed all the time. However, if one of you is consistently putting more into the relationship than the other, this will create a severe imbalance. For example, if you feel that it is always down to you to suggest things to do, or it's you who generally takes the initiative, then your relationship isn't equal. In some cases you might even feel that without your energy and input the relationship would fall apart.

If you don't feel that you and your partner are contributing equally to your relationship, then sooner or later this will lead to severe resentment. If you are the one who does all the giving and none – or very little – of the receiving, you are putting yourself into sacrifice. Going into sacrifice means that you are willing to abandon your own life, friends and interests for the sake of being with your partner. When you do this you lose your sense of self, and you and your relationship suffer. If your partner expects you to give up what's important to you and the things that you enjoy, then they are not honouring or supporting you.

Many of us avoid intimacy altogether because we are afraid of going into sacrifice and losing ourselves in the relationship. Often this originates in early childhood with some kind of emotional loss which was never resolved and as a result we remain resolutely independent, even when in a relationship. For a relationship to thrive we need to move into interdependence so that each person can enjoy the mutual benefits of being together. It takes courage to do this because it involves acknowledging all of the suppressed and repressed feelings which we have dissociated from. Being willing to reconnect with those painful places in us and heal them ultimately sets us free and creates the potential for a joyful and equal partnership.

Why do we create unequal relationships?

We create unequal relationships when we fear both our potential greatness and our presumed inadequacy. So few of us really give ourselves permission to be all of who we can be and grow into our full stature. And by the same token, we fear that we aren't good enough and that we are unequal to the task of becoming our very best. The ability to create an equal relationship depends entirely

> the ability to create an equal relationship depends entirely on how you feel about yourself

on how you feel about yourself. If you go into a relationship feeling less confident, intelligent, accomplished and lovable than your partner, you are starting the relationship on an unequal footing.

So, how do you know whether you are currently in an equal relationship or if your past relationships have been based on equality or not?

brilliant action

First, ask yourself whether you have ever been in a relationship in which you or your partner:

- had more power or control;
- had more money;
- was much more experienced or accomplished;
- was more self-confident;
- had more needs;
- had more of a tendency to give;
- was more willing to commit.

Have you answered yes to any of the above questions? If so, have you been aware of these imbalances? How did they make you feel? Have you tended to recreate these imbalances with each new partner?

Now consider the following questions, which are intended to give you a deeper insight into any dependency issues in your relationships. If you are not currently in a relationship, focus on a past relationship.

- In which areas do you feel dependent on your partner?
- How do your dependencies manifest?
- Is there anything that you ask your partner to do for you that you need to be doing for yourself? If so, what is it?
- In which ways is your partner dependent on you?

- Who is more emotionally dependent on the other?
- Are you taking on the responsibility for the emotional well-being of your partner at the expense of your own?
- Who do you feel is the stronger of the two of you, in terms of being able to ask for what you want?
- Which one of you expresses a stronger need to be in control? Who usually gets their way in terms of making choices and taking decisions?
- Which one of you is/feels more successful or fulfilled in their career?
- Does one of you have more control of your sexual relationship?
- Are you happy with the status quo and, if not, how would you like it to change?

Notice how you feel as you explore the above questions. Is there anything that you would like to change? Write down your thoughts and spend some time considering the impact that any imbalances have on your sense of self and your relationship. Which ones would you most like to change?

Stay in your power

When you are in a relationship with someone you perceive as being better than you in some way – whether you consider them more intelligent, successful, attractive or confident – you give your power away. As soon as you do that, you are in effect diminishing yourself and giving out the message that you aren't good enough and therefore not worthy of your partner's love and respect. When that happens you are more likely to allow yourself to be dominated or taken for granted. So what factors are at work in our psyches when we fail to create a balanced dynamic in our relationships? And how do we tip the scales and give away our power?

When you love and accept yourself, you are much more likely to be attracted to someone who has an equally positive self-regard. This enables you to discuss and negotiate the terms of your relationship knowing that you are both individuals in your own right, with a healthy respect for yourselves and each other. As long as there is respect, reciprocity and real communication between you, it's possible to resolve even the most difficult issues that arise.

Having a clear sense of yourself empowers you and enables you to set healthy boundaries in your relationships. Real power has no need to dominate and control, and empowered people aren't afraid of being in relationships with other equally powerful people. In fact they positively welcome it, because they know how dynamic, passionate, exciting and stimulating it is. Real power means that you know who you are in your core and that you exist in your own right. It means that you are rooted in your own centre of gravity and enjoy the interplay and balance of power between you and your partner. Virtually all of us have the potential to achieve this kind of relationship, but first we have to acknowledge our vulnerabilities and the parts of us that we are afraid of fully expressing.

> real power has no need to dominate and control

Our positive self-concepts can sometimes hide some quite negative and painful feelings about ourselves. Often we mask our fear, sense of inadequacy or feelings of inferiority behind a façade that may be diametrically opposed to who we really are. For example, we might present ourselves as the tough guy, when deep down we feel scared or even cowardly. Or we might exaggerate our accomplishments and appear to be more confident than we really are. Our vulnerabilities and painful experiences can create defensive behaviours as we attempt to protect ourselves from our uncomfortable feelings and unhealed parts. As we develop more protective layers, we are in effect running away from our true identity. And when we dissemble we deny ourselves the possibility of an honest and equal relationship.

 **brilliant** action

Take a look at the following statements and decide which ones you agree with. Notice how these beliefs make you feel, and give yourself some time to consider how these affirmations might impact on the quality of your relationships.

Attitudes that create equal relationships	Attitudes that create unequal relationships
I expect you to make me feel happy/good about myself	I take responsibility for my own happiness and well-being
I expect you to stop me from feeling lonely	Be my companion and let us respect each other's need for space and time alone
I'm stronger/more intelligent/accomplished, so therefore I hold the power in the relationship	We acknowledge and value each other's differences and seek to address and resolve any issues between us
It's my way or the highway/I always give in to you	We discuss and negotiate and value what each other has to say
I am completely dependent on you	We both have a strong sense of self and have a moderate dependency on each other
You are responsible for meeting my needs	We meet some of each other's needs
I expect you always to be there for me and never let me down	I trust that we will always do our best, but know that we are human and fallible
I don't expect to be loved/ supported/ respected	I deserve to be loved/supported/respected
I look to you for a feeling of stability and security	Our relationship supports and enriches my inner stability

Risk being vulnerable

For many of us, the fear of showing ourselves for who we really are can set up a barrier to creating close, mutually satisfying relationships. Our intimate relationships connect us with our deepest vulnerabilities and fears of being rejected, abandoned or not loved in the way in which we expect to be. If we have experienced any of these painful scenarios then we may interpret what happened to us as an indication that there is something wrong with us. As a result we will often doubt our ability to create happy, equal and committed relationships. Our self-doubt prevents us from saying what we truly feel and believe and opening ourselves up to our partner. We may even withhold love, if we fear that it can't or won't be reciprocated. In actual fact, it is our self-rejection, self-abandonment and lack of love for *ourselves* that often perpetuates our unhappy relationships. This translates into negative self-talk such as 'I'm not attractive/interesting/accomplished enough to hold this person's interest, and sooner or later they will move on to somebody better'.

The truth is that sooner or later all of us need to risk being vulnerable if we want to create a relationship that is alive, passionate and real. Fear can even be useful as long as we are not driven or stopped by it, since it connects us with where we are hiding or keeping ourselves small. Of course it hurts when our partner breaks off a relationship or isn't willing to commit. It can also feel painful when we are the one feeling half-hearted or doing the leaving. It's not easy seeing someone else's upset or disappointment. But if we get stuck in our fear of being hurt or of hurting someone else, we'll never fully engage and bring all of ourselves to the relationship. When both you and your partner are willing to match each other and be completely honest and wholehearted you can build a fulfilling relationship based on equality and mutuality.

> when we are afraid to be ourselves we deprive both ourselves and our partners

When we are afraid to be ourselves, afraid to be wholly responsible for who we are, we deprive both ourselves and our partners. Although taking responsibility for ourselves can be immensely challenging, it is the greatest gift we can bring to our relationships. And when you commit to your own authenticity, you care and honour yourself and your relationship.

An equal relationship is one in which both partners:

- feel that they have a full and balanced life;
- are able to give and take;
- support the other's growth without feeling threatened;
- complement each other by making up for one another's weaknesses;
- know who they are and what supports them;
- are authentic;
- value co-operation rather than competition;
- are committed to help each other learn and grow.

In an equal relationship neither partner tries to change the other or uses their strengths to intimidate or make their partner feel inadequate. The love and acceptance that you experience in an equal partnership is based on mutuality and reciprocity, and allows you and your partner to be the very best you can be.

brilliant action

Complete the following sentences without censoring yourself. Just see what spontaneously comes up for you.

- What scares me most about being all of who I am in a relationship is ...
- In my experience, men are ...

- In my experience, women are ...

- What I risk most by opening myself up to someone is ...

- What I stand to gain by being myself/fully engaging in a relationship is ...

- Being in an equal relationship means ...

Take some time to consider your answers. What have your responses revealed? What can you learn from them?

Making decisions

How do you and your partner make decisions? Does one of you tend to take the lead, or do you discuss each decision until you reach a compromise? When you make any decision, it's essential to take the feelings and opinions of both of you into account. Some decisions will be easier to negotiate than others, but when you listen to each other's perspective and keep talking until you reach an agreement then you are both sharing the decision-making process and reinforcing the equality in your relationship. Sometimes, one or other of you might feel more informed and therefore better equipped to make the decision. If you do defer to your partner's experience or knowledge, make sure that you listen to your intuition to check whether the right decision has been made. If something doesn't sit right with you, voice your concern and open up the discussion again.

Sometimes it can be quite challenging to arrive at a consensus, particularly when it comes to our values and what we feel we can't compromise on. It might be something emotionally complex, like when to start a family or how much contact to have with difficult family members. Or it might be on a more practical level, such as who takes responsibility for the day-to-day running of the household. It's important to remember that your viewpoints aren't right or wrong, they're just different. By sharing your viewpoints and being open to each other's thinking and feelings you can move forward. No matter how differently you see a particular situation, there will almost always be something that the other can appreciate and accept. Keep exploring and discovering as much as you can about where you are both coming from so that you can better understand and value each other.

In the end, all relationships involve compromise, but what's important is that each person remains true to their values and maintains their integrity. The balance of power between you and your partner isn't static and will ebb and flow. The secret is never to lose sight of who you are and always to accept that you and your partner deserve equal recognition, acceptance and love.

brilliant tip

When it comes to making decisions, remember that there is no right or wrong, just different perspectives. Keep talking and make sure that you reach an agreement with which you are both happy.

brilliant action

Is there an issue over which you and your partner aren't able to agree? Try to answer the following questions:

- What do you and your partner disagree about?
- What would a compromise feel like for each of you?
- What could get in the way of reaching a compromise?
- What would happen if you did agree to compromise?
- What would it feel like?

 **example**

Create a balanced and equal relationship

Penny and Ali had communicated well when they first met and shared much of themselves with each other. But after a few months it became apparent that there were taboo areas that Ali didn't want to discuss about himself. He'd had a difficult childhood and had two failed marriages, and Penny wanted to know more about what had happened and how these experiences had impacted on him. Penny felt hurt that Ali had put up a brick wall but when she tried to encourage him to open up he either detached from her or lost his temper. At first, Penny continued to be very warm and loving with Ali and hoped that he would respond in kind but he felt threatened by the intimacy that she was seeking and continued to shut her out. As a last resort, Penny asked Ali whether he would be willing for them to have some couples coaching and he agreed. I suggested seeing Ali for some individual sessions and over time he gradually allowed his vulnerability to come to the surface and connect with his repressed emotions from the past. This had a very positive effect on their relationship and gave them a foundation on which to build trust and intimacy. Their relationship transformed and they now enjoy a wonderfully open and transparent loving relationship.

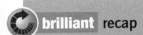 **recap**

Each of us is unique, and when we accept and value our differences we create a feeling of respect and equality in our relationships. This is essential if we are to thrive and feel happy and cherished. If we try to change our partners, or change ourselves to please our partners, our relationships become out of balance. When you create an equal relationship based on mutuality and reciprocity, you and your partner are at your best.

🔍 brilliant task for the week

Think about all the couples you know. How many of them have what you consider to be an equal relationship? Keep thinking about what being in an equal relationship means to you, and write down all your thoughts.

CHAPTER 9

Let go of
the past

Life is a series of natural and spontaneous changes. Don't resist them – that only creates sorrow. Let reality be reality. Let things flow naturally forward in whatever way they like.

Lao-Tse, philosopher and founder of Taoism

Whenever we start a new relationship we bring our personal history with us. Some of us may feel that we've wiped the slate clean, let the past go and moved on by the time we meet someone new, while others may still bear the scars of a broken heart. However many times we may have loved and lost, what's important is how we come through these experiences and our attitude towards them.

The end of a relationship, as we have seen in Chapter 4, can be devastating, and losing someone you love can be one of the most painful and traumatic experiences of our lives. Even when we have made the choice to move on, the decision to do so can still be fraught with angst and difficulty. Everyone reacts to loss and the end of a relationship differently. Some people grieve the past and find it extremely hard to let go, while others go into denial and pretend that everything is fine, thinking that ignoring their pain will make it go away. Another common reaction to a break-up is anger, and this can be particularly toxic when we hold on to it and bring it into a new relation-ship. Some people close down and vow never to get emotionally involved again. Letting go of the past counters the negative – and sometimes destructive – influence of holding on. In fact, it is critical to let go in order to be emotionally available to a new relationship. And it is not only a question of letting go of a partner or old patterns. It's also important to let go of old parts of you which no longer define you as a person.

Sooner or later, the time comes when we meet someone new to whom we are attracted and we find ourselves getting involved again. The success of that new relationship will partly depend on how you have resolved the past and come to terms with it. If you are still holding on to unresolved grief, anger or resentment from the past, this will inevitably poison your chances of future happiness.

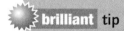 **brilliant** tip

Holding on decreases your chances of attracting a new relationship. Letting go enhances your attractiveness and makes you more magnetic.

Recognising ambivalence

Sometimes there are good reasons to be afraid of getting involved with someone or becoming more intimate with an existing partner, but there are also some dubious reasons too. So it's important that you are very aware of your motives whenever you are tempted to pull away from a partner or a potential relationship. Otherwise, fear – in the guise of your rational voice – is liable to get the better of you.

We are not always in touch with our fears. Although some of them are conscious, others become buried and relegated to our unconscious. Our unconscious fears are potentially more serious stumbling blocks to creating a happy and fulfilling relationship. When our fear gets buried we might appear to want an intimate relationship and even consciously desire one, while simultaneously sabotaging that from happening. This kind of ambivalence is often rooted in a past hurt and it's essential that we understand how this prevents us from having a loving relationship. So, if you feel as if you're doing everything you possibly can to attract a new partner or to make an existing rela-

> it's possible you are allowing the past to undermine your heart's desire

tionship work but without success, it's possible you are allowing the past to undermine your heart's desire.

Let's say that something in you is holding back from getting emotionally involved with someone. Your conscious reservations about becoming more intimate and committed may be very clear to you. For example, you might decide that you aren't emotionally ready to commit to someone and that you need to cultivate your independence. This might well be the case. Equally, your rationale could be a strategy to protect yourself from feeling vulnerable again. It isn't always easy to tell whether our reservations about a relationship are well founded, or simply a fear of being hurt. Deep down we almost certainly know what really feels true. However, it's important that we explore our reservations and discover what is best for us.

brilliant action

The only way to resolve any ambivalence you might have about relationships is to allow your fears to come into awareness. However, this is easier said than done. It takes courage, willingness and persistence to unearth our old buried hurts and disappointments and acknowledge them for what they are. You can start the process by making a list of what you think you might be afraid of where intimacy and commitment

▶

are concerned. Come up with as many drawbacks to being in an intimate relationship that you can think of, and write down any negative outcomes you think there might be. For example, you might believe that being in love makes you feel needy and dependent and, according to your past experience, that pushes people away. Complete the following sentence and come up with as many examples as you can.

I am afraid of being in an intimate relationship because:

1

2

3

4

5

Did any of your answers surprise you? How many of your fears do you feel are based on your past experience? Would you be willing to let go of your fears and create a more open, receptive attitude towards being in a relationship?

Break the cycle

Of course, even when you've become aware of your fears about relationships, you may still feel that history will repeat itself. It's easy to believe that your fear serves to protect you from making the same mistakes and that your wary attitude will keep you from getting hurt. In actual fact, the opposite is true. Whatever we expect is likely to become a self-fulfilling prophecy. For example, if you have a negative expectation about being let down in a relationship it's likely that you'll create what you most fear. To help you break this cycle, mentally emphasise to yourself that not *everyone* is, for example, unreliable or commitment-phobic. This will enable you to be more open to a different kind of experience and expect the best from people you meet. As you shift your focus from your fears to the positive qualities you want to attract into your life and your relationships, you will create a new template. Releasing the past means you can express the real you that's been hiding beneath your fears and it will free you to give and receive love.

brilliant action

The challenges and problems in your previous relationship(s) are good guides for finding out how much you've moved on and what you learnt from these experiences. Make a list of your previous relationship(s) and then answer the questions below. As you consider each one individually you might see a pattern emerging.

- What was the purpose of this relationship?
- What worked best?
- What didn't work?
- How did you grow in this relationship?
- What lessons have you learned?
- What did you heal?
- What are you still holding on to?
- What, if anything, is there to forgive?
- What gifts did you bring to the relationship?
- What gifts did you receive?
- What is your prevalent attitude to being in an intimate, committed relationship?
- Does your current attitude help or hinder your ability to be in a loving relationship?
- What, if anything, do you need to let go of from the past?
- Are you willing to do that?

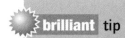 **tip**

As you shift your focus from your fears to the positive qualities you want to attract into your life and your relationships, you will create a new template.

Take responsibility for your anger

Do you feel angry towards your partner or an ex-partner? We usually have all kinds of good reasons to justify our anger, but what we aren't usually aware of is the fact that our anger often masks much deeper, painful feelings within us, such as hurt, fear, guilt, rejection, loss, frustration, disappointment and sadness. Anger can, of course, be legitimate and we need to know the difference between healthy anger and the kind of anger that is destructive and which we project on to others. Clean anger that arises in response to a violation of our values or boundaries, for example, gives a very clear message about how we are feeling in response to that infringement. This kind of anger isn't the kind that festers and once expressed we can normally let go of it.

> anger often masks much deeper, painful feelings within us

When we mask our anger it has nowhere to go but inwards. Unexpressed anger has a toxic effect on both the mind and the body and can manifest as headaches, ulcers, nervous conditions, depression, a feeling of impotence or self-destructive behaviour. The other costs of masked anger are not getting what you want and feelings of low self-esteem. At the other end of the scale is sudden anger. This can happen when you deny your anger – either because you don't like it in yourself or others – until the pressure builds to an intolerable level and you explode. A less dramatic coping strategy for unresolved or unexpressed anger avoids direct confrontation altogether. One of you may appear to go along with what your partner is saying and seem to co-operate but never actually do what is asked of you or what you seemingly agree to. For example, you might forget to make a phone call, put off an important job or perpetuate a behaviour which you said you'd change. Psychologists call this passive-aggressive behaviour. While positive anger clears the air, passive aggression hangs around, poisoning the atmosphere and the relationship.

When we communicate our anger in a conscious way rather than use it as a weapon, we can move through it much more easily. However, unresolved anger from the past is much more insidious. It can sometimes be an attempt to project on to others our own unresolved feelings about ourselves, pretending that our anger has nothing to do with us. An effective way to move through our anger can be to ask ourselves: 'What is the feeling underneath my anger?' You may not get an immediate sense of what it is, but be willing to keep asking the question until you drop into the deeper feeling that the anger is masking. This can be powerful emotional work and you may choose to work with a counsellor or therapist to help you connect with any emotions which you have denied or repressed. Get as much support as you need, and know that this process is for your own healing and well-being.

 **brilliant** action

If you are currently in a relationship, think about any areas of conflict between you and your partner that create anger and resentment in you. Is there a particular area in which you feel stuck and afraid to move forward? Would you be willing to change your perception about this situation? If the answer is yes, then first you will need to forgive either your partner or yourself – or both – for the pain you're experiencing, and set yourself free. ▶

Once we forgive, we are in flow again and we can open ourselves to being in a loving relationship with ourselves and our partners.

Make a list of all the reasons and justifications that you think you have for holding on to anger or resentment. Then consider the following questions.

● Has this been a pattern in your life?

● Consider where you have been seeing your partner as wrong, bad or guilty. Is there anything for which you are judging or blaming your partner? If so, give examples.

● Is there anything for which you are judging or blaming yourself?

● How does this affect your relationship?

Our anger can also be in response to our feelings of helplessness or humiliation. We can summon anger to protect us from heartache, jealousy, sadness or rejection. When we recognise this and take responsibility for our emotions, we can begin to communicate with greater honesty and integrity. As you begin to acknowledge any powerful emotions that you haven't expressed, you free yourself to experience deeper and more loving relationships. Be gentle with yourself and, if necessary, find someone you trust to help you open up the full spectrum of your inner feelings.

brilliant example

Don't mask your true feelings

Amy admitted that she'd always been fiery by nature, but ever since she and Hugo had been together her anger had got worse. Every time they had a disagreement about something Amy would get disproportionately angry with Hugo, and he was left feeling hurt and confused. Hugo confessed that he often felt that Amy was spoiling for a fight and so he had started to distance himself from her both emotionally and sexually. As we discussed their situation, it became apparent that Amy was feeling very upset but wasn't allowing herself to express her emotions. Gradually, as she began to feel that it was safe for her to open up and that she wouldn't be judged, she revealed that she had always lived in constant terror of being vulnerable in a relationship. Two years before she had met Hugo, her fiancé had broken off their engagement and told her it was because he'd met someone else. Amy was devastated, but her way of dealing with this painful rejection was to throw herself into work and keep busy. She buried all her hurt and thought she'd moved on, until she got into a relationship with Hugo. Her deep fear that men weren't to be trusted had created a powerful anger in Amy and each time she felt afraid she would project that on to Hugo.

In spite of feeling very vulnerable, Amy felt a huge sense of relief at being able to open up to her fears and share them with Hugo. She agreed that each time she felt threatened in their relationship, instead of defending herself with anger, she would simply state how she was feeling. She and Hugo grew much closer as Amy learnt to trust herself enough to be open with him. She no longer pushed him away with her anger, and their relationship was transformed.

Forgive and let go

The ability to heal past wounds and forgive others – and ourselves – is essential if we are to move on and create happy and fulfilling relationships. When we heal our past wounds we reconcile ourselves with our personal history and are at peace. When we don't make peace with ourselves and our past, it continues to plague us and so our unresolved issues spill out into our next relationship. Holding on to old negative emotions about our ex-partner(s) has an adverse effect on us emotionally, physically and spiritually, and keeps us prisoners of our past and our pain. We are unable to move forward and establish healthy and happy relationships with others – or indeed ourselves. Holding on to anger, for example, can be very self-

> the more we rerun our old hurts and disappointments, the more stuck we become in the past

destructive, as it keeps reinforcing our negative feelings and stops us from giving and receiving love. When you relive and constantly think about past situations that you still feel angry about, you are never free to move on. And the more we rerun our old hurts and disappointments, the more stuck we become in the past.

Often our negative feelings are based on disappointment and the pain of unfulfilled expectations. The truth is that however badly treated or let down we may feel, until we resolve these feelings and let them go we will never be able to fully and wholeheartedly engage in another relationship. Not only that, but we are likely to project our unresolved issues on to a new partner, making them the scapegoat for what essentially belongs to us.

It isn't easy to forgive, especially if the hurt runs deep. Forgiveness may not always happen at once, it can take a while. It's often a process and we may have to keep forgiving the same person in our hearts again and again until we've let go of the hurt. When we forgive we are choosing not to hurt back or to make the other person pay. Part of us may want to get our own back but when we forgive we override these impulses.

By forgiving others for their perceived transgressions, we are not condoning their behaviour. We are simply deciding to take responsibility for our own healing and release ourselves from all the painful emotions we attach to that person. In the process, we might also become more aware of our own part in what happened and forgive ourselves for whatever we did or didn't do. Forgiveness doesn't require that we make contact with our ex-partner(s). It can be an internal process in which we mentally and emotionally let go of the pain, emotion and resentment that we have attached to them. When we are able to do this, we free ourselves from the past and give ourselves the gift of being happy in the present.

It's not always an ex-partner we need to forgive. Sometimes we feel aggrieved by the words or actions of our current partner. Forgiveness is extremely powerful and will allow you to transform difficulties in your relationships. It will help you resolve conflicts and change your perception of others, seeing them in a new light. The gift of forgiveness is that it releases us from patterns in which we are caught. It releases us from victim mentality and getting stuck in situations that make us unhappy. Make it your intention to move on with your life and let go of everything that is holding you back.

 **brilliant** action

- Write a letter to yourself focusing on anything you need to forgive yourself for. Remind yourself that you are human, and therefore – like everyone else – you make mistakes. Be kind and compassionate with yourself and resist the temptation to be judgemental.

- Make a list of the people you would like to forgive. You might want to write a letter to each person without necessarily intending to send it. Remember that one of the criteria for having a healthy relationship with your partner is to have resolved the past. Each time you let go of a negative emotion, you are one step closer to getting your life back and enjoying a loving relationship with both yourself and your partner.

Release guilt

Often we carry guilt about the way in which we behaved towards a partner. When we look back at our past and really assess what happened, we begin to realise that there are many reasons for our words and actions. While feeling guilty can be a normal response, it doesn't actually resolve anything and isn't a viable solution. It's only when we are able to stand back and contemplate our past with compassion that we are able to see that there is much more to what we did and said than we realise. For example, you may regret losing your temper and saying hurtful things that you didn't mean. But it's possible that you were simply trying to protect yourself and did the best you could at the time. Or it might be that you didn't see any other way of dealing with the situation and acted in the heat of the moment. Perpetuating your negative feelings will only make you feel worse. It is only by forgiving ourselves and transforming our negative feelings that we can release any guilt we have about the past.

Giving ourselves permission to feel at peace with our past actions is one of the most positive steps we can take towards living a life free from regrets, disappointments and guilt. The more we are able to accept both the light and the dark in ourselves and let go of our harsh judgements and criticisms, the more available we become for a loving relationship. Forgiveness can be challenging, and requires that we open our hearts and become bigger than our desire to blame and shame. But when you forgive either your partner or yourself – or both – for the pain you're experiencing, you set yourself free.

> giving ourselves permission to feel at peace with our past actions is one of the most positive steps we can take

Let go of blame

We all share the same need to be loved and nurtured. When we state our needs rather than blame others for not fulfilling them, we create an authentic intimacy with our partner. If, however, we use blame or criticism to cover up needs that we haven't expressed or which haven't been met, we create distance and conflict. Blaming others can often be a refusal to take responsibility for our own happiness. No matter how often we attempt to make our partner responsible for our happiness, for example by guilt-tripping or coercing them, it cannot ever happen. In fact, giving someone else responsibility for our happiness is tantamount to condemning ourselves to being miserable.

If you are feeling blame towards your partner for anything, try expressing whatever it is that you need from them instead. Rather than adopting an accusatory tone and saying 'It was wrong of you to ...', reframe this statement to 'I'd like you to listen/acknowledge me/pay more attention to me'. Stating clearly what you need empowers you and is less likely to put your partner on the defensive. Next time you are tempted to accuse your partner of being wrong, step back and check in with what it is that you really need from them or the situation. As you shift your energy, your whole attitude will change and create a very different outcome.

brilliant tip

When we state our needs rather than blame others for not fulfilling them, we create an authentic intimacy with our partner.

Feel the feelings

One of the reasons why we sometimes find it hard to release our negative emotions is because we don't always want to feel them. We sometimes shut down our painful feelings and as a consequence we lose touch with these parts of ourselves. And if we don't accept and integrate our darker emotions, they will seep out into our relationships in an unconscious and sometimes destructive way.

Often our resistance to exploring our past is because we fear that it will bring up the painful feelings and memories that we have tried so hard to forget. However, if we are willing to take a risk and acknowledge and address our bottled-up feelings, our lives and our relationships become more enriched and authentic. Being open with your partner enables them to understand you better and to become part of your healing process. Any relationship worth having requires a commitment to honest communication, and this includes sharing your past emotional wounds and how they impact on the quality of your relationship. Acknowledging and accepting our feelings is necessary in order to live fully in the present, without prejudgements or unrealistic expectations.

As you reflect on how your life can benefit from letting go of the past, remember that this process is important for you and your own happiness. Be gentle and compassionate with yourself: letting go of your past occurs gradually but it will inevitably transform your life – and your relationships – for the better.

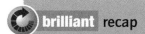 **brilliant** recap

We all carry some baggage from the past. This can include painful feelings such as anger, resentment, guilt, sadness, fear, disappointment and regret. When we don't acknowledge these feelings we can't love wholeheartedly or enjoy true intimacy and commitment. Although it takes time and courage to honour our more negative emotions, doing so sets us free and enables us to be fully in the present.

brilliant task for the week

As you resolve to unburden your heart and free your mind of old grievances, be aware of how it feels to hold on to these painful emotions. And ask yourself the following questions:

- Am I willing to let go of the past?
- If not, what will it take for me to do that?
- How does it make me feel to hold on to fear, anger, guilt or resentment?
- What impact does this have on me and my relationships?
- Am I willing to accept and forgive and commit to my future happiness?

CHAPTER 10

See your relationship as a work in progress

It is not until you have the courage to engage in human relationships that you grow.

Gary Zukav, best-selling author

It's easy to fall in love. But it can be a lot harder to stay in love. There are lots of reasons for this. Sometimes it's simply because we evolve in different ways from our partners and outgrow each other. The passion and the aliveness we once experienced in the relationship just aren't there anymore – the connection between us no longer feels so compelling and we fall out of love. At other times the challenge of working through the issues that we inevitably experience in our relationships seems too daunting. As a result, we hold back from telling the complete truth about our feelings, push down our emotions and drift apart.

When you are connected to your partner you are able to share and experience each other's feelings. When that connection is broken you feel alienated and distant from each other. Some couples choose to continue their relationship even when they have lost their connection and mutual attraction, but in the process they sacrifice the opportunity to keep growing and learning from each other. So how do you stay connected and why is this so integral to the health and success of your relationship?

There's no way you can absolutely ensure that any relationship will last but there are many ways to preserve the love you have and rekindle it if it has started to fade. Relationships need to be nurtured if they are to stay alive, and your relationship maintenance deserves at least as much effort and time as the other aspects of your life. Working at a relationship doesn't necessarily mean that it's in trouble. Think of it more like tending a well-kept garden so that everything in it thrives and flourishes. A relationship that you consciously work at is likely to be pleasurable, fulfilling and rewarding, despite the bumpy moments. Conversely, ignoring or denying what isn't working or blithely assuming that everything is fine can create stress, resentment and a breakdown in communication. Enjoying the good times as well as being willing to tackle the difficult issues when they arise will give your relationship balance and depth. And empower you and your partner with increasing confidence in your ability to grow and mature your relationship.

> working at a relationship doesn't necessarily mean that it's in trouble

**brilliant** tip

See your relationship as something that needs to be cultivated in order to stay alive and thrive. The more you nurture your relationship, the more it will grow.

Become familiar with your buttons

We've all had the experience of having someone snap at us, seemingly out of nowhere. No matter how self-aware we are or how close we are to our partners, we can still react to what we perceive as a judgemental, hurtful or critical remark.

This usually happens when one of our buttons gets pushed. Buttons are like tender spots that symbolise wounds that need to be acknowledged and healed. When our buttons get pushed, an emotional reaction is triggered in us. It may be a situation that reminds us of the past and which touches a vulnerable place in us. For example, if you were criticised as a child, you may fly off the handle if your partner says something negative about you. Getting your buttons pushed can cause you to react angrily, feel deeply hurt, fearful or depressed.

Each of us will have our own trigger points depending on our life experiences and individual temperaments. For some of us our Achilles heel might be a remark about our physical appearance, for others it might be an accusation of being untruthful or untrustworthy. Getting emotionally triggered can feel bewildering for both parties and, if not properly handled, the strong feelings that are unleashed can escalate into a full-scale argument. Knowing what our buttons are, taking responsibility for the pain behind them and sharing this with our partner can help us to heal or resolve those vulnerable and highly sensitive places in us.

brilliant action

Do you know what triggers your buttons? Make a list of these and, if it feels right, share one or two with your partner. If your partner seems to be receptive and sympathetic, you may wish to share your whole list, explaining why these things upset you so much. If your partner is willing, you can ask them to make their own button list and share it with you. It obviously requires a great deal of trust to share this information, so if you don't feel you have established this kind of trust with your partner, you may initially prefer to write your list for yourself.

▶

The things that push my buttons are:

1

2

3

4

Learn to collaborate

Each of us functions according to our own timetable. Our priorities concerning what we want to do and when we want to do it don't always coincide with the priorities of our partner. When we're in synch with our partners our relationships flow and have a sense of ease. But what happens when our timetables clash? Partners who are out of synch can find it challenging to stay connected, reconcile their differences and find a shared solution that genuinely takes both of their needs and desires into account. Even when the fit between you and your partner is very good, there may still be conflicts to resolve. Your values and vision of a shared future may mirror your partner's, yet when it comes to living out the details significant differences can emerge. You may both want a child, for example, but find yourselves at loggerheads about the timing. One of you may feel a burning desire to become a parent while the other doesn't feel ready. To resolve such conflicts, you need to strengthen your ability to collaborate.

The word 'collaborate' comes from the Latin meaning 'to work together'. Working together means being willing to listen to each other and address the issues between you. When you collaborate you have a much better chance of creating a mutually agreeable outcome. Collaboration enables you to strengthen the feeling of 'we'. Of course, that may mean letting go of previous ideas about what you will or won't do and what you will and won't give in on. And it does require flexibility and being willing to compromise – a compromise that meets your shared needs as a couple. However, when you are willing to do this you create the potential to grow together in ways you may not expect.

Each couple will have their own unique dynamic and there isn't one single solution to the crises and dilemmas we encounter in relationships. But if you are committed to a shared future, it's important to find shared solutions rather than individual ones. Seeing the whole as greater than the sum of the parts can motivate you to go beyond your individual wants and needs and discover what is best for your relationship. In fact, it can be the saving grace of your relationship. Even if you feel that you know best, true

> it's important to find shared solutions rather than individual ones

solutions are more likely to be found jointly than individually. Collaborating with your partner means that rather than expect or demand that everything works out on your terms as individuals, you find a way through together.

brilliant action

Think about an issue that needs to be resolved or a decision that you and your partner are experiencing difficulty agreeing on and that you would like to work through together. Take it in turns to express your different points of view. And then ask yourselves whether you can understand, empathise or agree with anything your partner is saying. Before you start, answer the following questions:

● What issue do we want to discuss?

● Are we willing to let go of our positions and be open to another perspective?

▶

- Are we willing and able to respect the other's point of view?
- Can we accept that there is no right or wrong, just different opinions?
- Is it our intention to arrive at a mutually agreeable outcome?

Once you've answered and discussed the above, you can go on to asking each other the following questions:

- What is most important to you?
- What would help me to understand your point of view better?
- What is important to you about maintaining your position?
- What would be your ideal solution to this situation?

It may take a while to work through these questions so be patient and don't give up if either of you becomes resistant or defensive. However intense or upsetting it can be to challenge yourselves and each other in this way, staying committed to your intention to work through your issue will help you ultimately to create a mutually beneficial outcome. In the process, you might be surprised by what you learn about yourselves and each other and how much more empathy and understanding is created between you. All of which will serve to deepen and strengthen your relationship.

Share your needs with each other

It can feel deeply stressful and frustrating when your partner isn't understanding or supportive of what you want or need, and there may be times when you react to this by becoming more demanding or argumentative than usual. Your partner may react to this by going into defence – either by withdrawing or retaliating. This sets up a pattern in which you are resisting each other and what is happening between you. You'll know you're in resistance when you:

- become stuck or entrenched in a point of view and unwilling to negotiate an alternative perspective;

- feel threatened or fearful and respond by closing down, splitting off or overreacting;
- feel like blocking or avoiding your own or your partner's emotions.

Resisting what is happening between you and you partner can undermine and potentially sabotage your relationship. One of the ways in which you can break through this resistance is by specifically expressing and taking into account each other's needs. Asking each other what it is that you need can be immensely revealing and enable your relationship to go to a deeper and more authentic place.

Being aware of your needs in a relationship doesn't mean that you require your partner to behave in a specific way – that would mean controlling them. Expressing your needs is about you and what is important or even essential to your happiness and well-being. When you and your partner are receptive to each other's needs, you give each other room to grow and feel good about your relationship.

 **brilliant** action

It's not always easy to find the right time to talk about your relationship with your partner. Sometimes you just have to seize the moment and blurt out what's on your mind. At other times you might prefer to arrange an appointed time when you know that you'll be able to give each other your undivided attention.

Once you've made the decision to open up, make sure that you express your feelings along with your underlying need, then make a specific request. For example: 'I'm feeling sad that we seem to be drifting apart and I need to spend some time with you so that we can talk about our relationship'.

 **example**

Express your needs

Nathan and Carmen had reached an impasse. They felt that they were essentially compatible but they kept coming up against the same issue. In the end, they decided to get some help. Carmen is a highly motivated woman and was busy forging her career when we met. As a result, she was often distracted and not focused on Nathan and their relationship. Nathan had suggested that they make more time for their relationship and although Carmen agreed, she never seemed to do anything about it. Nathan worked from home and although he too was very busy with work, he was mostly responsible for picking up the children from school and cooking supper. When we discussed this arrangement, Nathan expressed some resentment about the fact that Carmen seemed more interested in her career than their children, their home and their relationship. Although he really enjoyed being with their children, he felt that Carmen was taking him for granted. I asked them both to think about what they needed from each other and to communicate those needs clearly and without blaming or making demands. Some compromise was required as well as a renewed commitment to supporting each other in a mutually beneficial way. They found this process very useful and in a short time they were able to agree on a way of spending more time as a couple and as a family.

Couples often believe that if they've been together for a while, they should be able to read each other's minds. Although it can and does happen, no one should have to anticipate your needs, even if you think those needs should be obvious. If you want to take a healthy responsibility for your part of the relationship, always be willing to ask for what you need.

Become more intimate

There are lots of ways in which we become intimate with our partners: touching and connecting emotionally and physically, making love, being caring, walking hand in hand along a moonlit beach, enjoying a candlelit dinner and reading in bed together are just some of the ways in which we feel close and connected. But the single most powerful way of creating an intimate bond with each other is by revealing your inner life and showing your true self. The more deep inner truths you share with your partner, the more intimate you become. Of course this doesn't happen overnight. Opening ourselves up is a gradual process and it takes time and trust to drop through our defensive layers and disclose our innermost selves. Intimacy means being real with each other and showing your whole self, warts and all. To do that you will need to value and trust yourself enough to be able to be open.

> intimacy means being real with each other and showing your whole self

Intimacy and self-worth are inextricably linked. As you become more self-loving, you become more open and willing to share your self with another person. This openness allows you to be more intimate and more self-loving, thus creating a virtuous circle.

Intimacy isn't always about expressing yourself in words. It can often be non-verbal, such as looking into each other's eyes, holding each other's gaze, making love, listening to music together or giving each other a warm embrace. What's important is that you express what's in your heart and how you're feeling in the moment. Sharing feelings isn't always easy – even knowing what we are feeling can sometimes be difficult. But withholding them creates a barrier between you and your partner and makes intimacy impossible. So if you are genuinely confused or afraid of what you are feeling, share that with your partner and see what opens up. Self-disclosure is the starting point for genuine intimacy, and the experience of sharing deeply and honestly with your partner creates a strong bond between you.

For your relationship to thrive, you and your partner need to be well matched in your ability to be intimate. True intimacy means:

- being fully there for each other;
- being accepting of each other;
- being emotionally open;
- being present and attentive;
- taking delight in each other's presence;
- enjoying doing things together;
- being interested in and supportive of each other's growth and development;
- respecting each other's space;
- feeling confident in your overall closeness as a couple;
- being best friends.

brilliant tip

Be courageous and open enough to expose what is going on inside you and share your deeper selves with each other. The more open you and your partner are with each other, the more intimate you will become.

Cultivate your sensuality

Sex is one of the most sensual of all human experiences and a healthy and natural way for two people to communicate their love for each other. The sexual connection between you and your partner can unite you at a level of communication that can't be achieved in any other way, and bring your relationship to truly profound levels of intimacy. And the potent mixture of passion, trust and vulnerability that occurs in sexual intimacy can be the catalyst for expressing the deepest feelings one person can have for another.

The sexual intensity that occurs in the early stages of a relationship is very compelling. In such an emotionally charged state hormones run high and endorphins are released that act like stimulants. Not only that, but when you fall in love your serotonin levels increase, creating a strong feeling of happiness and well-being. It's easy to maintain sexual intensity at this stage, as the newness of the relationship and the chemistry combine to create a heightened sense of excitement. Over time, however, sexual routines become established and sex can become predictable and unexciting. Familiarity may not breed contempt, but it can sometimes lead to a cooling of your sexual attraction for each other.

If you relate to this, don't despair. You don't have to resign yourself to a mechanical or non-existent sex life or to ending the relationship in the hope of finding something more exciting. One way of reawakening your desire is by stimulating your *sensual* energy and appreciating the delights of each sense. Here are just a few ways in which to do that.

brilliant action

- Indulge your sense of touch by getting a massage, luxuriating in satin sheets, feeling the warmth and texture of your partner's skin.

- Enjoy listening to sensual music. Turn to nature and tune into the sound of the ocean or the rustling of the leaves in the trees. Sing your heart out.

▶

- Surround yourself with divine fragrances. Breathe in the intoxicating scent of a flower in bloom, or the mouth-watering smell of fresh coffee or deliciously cooked food.

- When you're eating, really savour each mouthful and enjoy the contrasts between sweet, bitter, savoury and spicy. Close your eyes to intensify the sensation. Excite your taste buds by being adventurous.

- Look at everything with the same wide-eyed-wonder that a child would. Look up at the stars sparkling in the night sky and witness the incredible beauty of the natural world. Make your home a sensual environment and surround yourself with things that are visually appealing to you.

Experiment with different ways of expanding your senses. Share these with your partner and don't be afraid to be adventurous. Cultivating your sensuality will help you to keep your relationship passionate and alive.

Tell the truth

Healing old emotional hurts is an ongoing process. When you are in a relationship with someone you feel safe with and loved by, feelings and emotions that you've been repressing or denying will often begin to surface in an attempt to be healed. You are much better equipped to deal with the inevitable tensions that arise between you and your partner if your relationship is honest, supportive and loving. Each time you and your partner get to a new level of intimacy in your relationship, there's an opportunity to heal another layer of repressed feelings. It might seem paradoxical that the more intimate you become with your partner, the more tension there can be between you. But this happens as you both risk greater vulnerability and honesty, and it is a normal response to becoming more open with each other. If you are committed to growth and a deeper connection with your partner, you will gradually learn to become more honest about your feelings, rather than hiding them from yourself and the person you love.

Telling the complete truth about how you feel can be difficult and painful but it is necessary if you truly want an honest and intimate relationship. Telling the truth means:

- asking for what you want when part of you would rather pretend that everything is fine;
- sharing your sadness or hurt when you'd rather protect yourself from it;
- admitting you've made a mistake when it would be easier to project the blame on to your partner;
- revealing secrets that you are reluctant or afraid to divulge.

Sharing how you're really feeling is a big part of what constitutes intimacy and what makes your relationship so valuable. You are much more likely to thrive as a couple if you don't hold back from each other or keep secrets. In fact, you become close precisely because you can totally and fully be yourselves with each other.

 **brilliant** action

Write down any secrets, feelings or information that you are withholding from your partner. Then write a few paragraphs about why you are holding back. After you have done that, choose a fairly minor secret, maybe something that you fear your partner wouldn't like or to which they might have a negative reaction. Find a time when you both feel relaxed and you won't be interrupted. Start by telling your partner your feelings about whatever it is that you're locking away. For example:

I want to be completely honest with you, although I am afraid that what I share with you is going to make you angry/upset/distant. However, I know that withholding from you by keeping it to myself is limiting our capacity to be really close.

If you want to open up to your partner but you feel too fearful of the consequences, you might think about enlisting the help of a therapist or a couple's counsellor. Don't be afraid to ask for help, as the health of your relationship could depend on it.

Accept the ebb and flow of your relationship

We are all paradoxical by nature and in relationships most of us have the need both to be together as well as have time alone. We all share a longing to connect deeply with others and yet we also need to honour our need for solitude, freedom and space. Each of us needs intimate connection and time away from our relationship to stay in touch with who we are. The need for autonomy is as important as the need to be close.

> the need for autonomy is as important as the need to be close

Coming to terms with and learning how to negotiate the basic poles of separateness and togetherness that exist in every relationship can be a challenge. When we acknowledge both sides, we become more whole and our relationships more healthy. Being in an intimate relationship while remaining true to ourselves can be an ongoing challenge. You and your partner are separate individuals with your own life stories, temperaments, preferences, rhythms and life paths. There will naturally be times when you are very connected and times when you feel more apart. Much like the tide ebbs and flows and the moon waxes and wanes, a relationship is a continuous flowing back and forth between joining and separating. The degree to which you are comfortable and accepting of this rhythmic flow will determine the health and success of your relationship.

Relationship v. individuality

As we discover more about ourselves we begin to define our-selves differently in our relationships. When we aren't really aware of ourselves it may be hard for us to know our partners intimately. But as we grow into ourselves and our relation-ships, we become more conscious of our individuality and how best to express it. Even though there are times when we merge with our partner, we will inevitably draw back into our own space again and the natural boundaries that exist between us. Boundaries protect us by keeping our definition of ourselves separate from the ideas others have about us. When we fall in love we open our boundaries to let our partner in and we let ourselves be included within our partner's boundaries. This means allowing our partner to become important enough to us to influence our sense of our own identity.

Ideally, when we are in an intimate relationship, we merge without allowing ourselves to be submerged or suffocated. Our boundaries can open, but they can also close as neces-sary to protect us. The ability to maintain flexible boundaries in this way depends on how well we know and accept who we really are. Self-knowledge and self-acceptance help us to use our boundaries flexibly. With flexible boundaries and a healthy capacity for merging, joining our lives means our sense of our-selves can grow larger. The challenge for each of us is to strike a balance between relationship and individuality, merging and self-definition.

Deepen your commitment

Being in a committed relationship involves both giving and receiving, working problems out and taking responsibility for the part you play. Even the best relationships have crisis points at certain stages, but these challenges, if consciously handled, can often lead to a renewed commitment. Losing your temper

196 brilliant relationships

with your partner doesn't mean that you stop loving each other. The give and take in a committed relationship enables us to let go of our insistence on being right, on getting our way, or competing and winning. That doesn't mean to say that we won't disagree with our partners or get into arguments, but when

focus on the common goals of your relationship and reaching agreements that work for both of you

we do the arguments don't need to last long and can end in resolution. Rather than use the argument as a way of expressing resentment or as a way of raking up the past, you can use the conflict between you as a way of helping to illuminate the deeper issues. Instead of demanding that your expectations be met, you focus on the common goals of your relationship and reaching agreements that work for both of you.

Quality time together

The warmth and tenderness we feel when we're close to someone we love increases our sense of trust and well-being. This can make it easier for us to risk exposing and confronting what we may have avoided before. Opening up to our partners brings us closer together, making us more willing to take further risks. If you are going to make a relationship work, you need to be present, both physically and emotionally, so that you can share companionship, conversation and affection. The pace of life these days means that we see less of each other. But you simply can't relate to someone if you're never together. So make sure that you prioritise each other. With planning it's possible to arrange quality time together.

If your relationship is worthwhile it's worth working on. Give it time. Keep up the communication. Never stop knowing that you deserve to be loved. Life is a process, and learning how to relate is a life-long process. You need to grow and let go, learn and expand, make mistakes and forgive. Take the risk of extending yourself. Don't take each other for granted. Truly be there for each other. If you're waiting for a relationship, be there for yourself. Look for opportunities to be encouraging and supportive, and try to be more present by listening, noticing and loving. Make it your intention to create a loving relationship. Express your hopes and dreams. Talk about what you appreciate in each other. Be curious about each other and get to know each other better. You might be surprised at how much more there is to discover.

 brilliant recap

For a relationship to grow and thrive, you need to be willing to take the risk of being more open, vulnerable, loving, committed, honest and courageous. This isn't always easy, but the rewards are great – both you and your relationship will grow beyond measure. Relationships are always evolving and there will be fresh challenges at each stage. See your lives together as a journey and the challenges as opportunities to deepen your connection with your partner and for you both to become more whole and happy.

brilliant task for the week

Practise being open and authentic in your conversations and intimate moments with your partner. Be really present and willing to fully engage, regardless of how uncomfortable this might feel at times.

CHAPTER 11

Live happily
ever after

Love is the power within us that affirms and values another human being as he or she is.
                    Robert A. Johnson, Jungian analyst and author

Love does not consist of gazing at each other, but of looking together in the same direction.
                    Antoine de Saint-Exupéry, novelist

Being in love is a blissful, magical and irresistible experience. It satisfies our need for a special connection with another human being, which brings intimacy, closeness and unconditional love. And on another level, it touches our lives with something numinous and gives them meaning. We feel more whole, more fully who we are. The honeymoon phase is exciting because it has so much potential and this stimulates a desire in us to perpetuate the feeling of extraordinary happiness. As our relationship progresses, however, we begin to realise that along with bringing us so much joy, love will bring up our issues and open us up to our vulnerable places. Each new relationship and stage of relationship brings fresh challenges, and we need to draw on all of our resources to fully engage with these. One of the secrets to having a brilliant relationship is working through the challenges that arise and seeing them as opportunities for growing and learning. As daunting as they can feel at times, without conflicts, differences, issues and dilemmas we wouldn't grow – either personally or in our relationships.

The obstacles that stand in the way of us creating a loving and committed relationship can be resolved. It's not always easy, and it takes willingness and motivation to keep pushing through our barriers and defences. And it takes courage to withdraw our projections, own them and consciously assimilate them into our psyches. But the more we take responsibility for ourselves and our personal journeys, the more our relationships will benefit. After all, the best relationship we can ever achieve with another person is directly related to the relationship we achieve with ourselves. You can't experience real joy and fulfilment in your relationship unless you recognise and honour your own intrinsic value. And when you believe that you're truly worthy of a loving relationship and that you deserve to be happy, that's what you will attract.

> the best relationship we can ever achieve with another person is directly related to the relationship we achieve with ourselves

Relationships work when you know how to make them work. It takes time to learn to trust your feelings and to put into practice all the experience and awareness that you have acquired along the way. The more you are able to do that, the more you can focus on loving each other and living your lives together. When you are in a loving relationship you feel desire for each other, enthusiasm for each other and deep affection towards each other. You see your lives together as something precious and enjoyable, and feel happy and grateful for what you have together. You actively acknowledge the important contribution your partner makes to your happiness and how much their affection and support means to you. And you're willing to do what it takes to heal any rifts that occur between you. You don't allow resentments to last long without working them through. And you don't withhold because of unexpressed anger from the past. You understand, accept and co-operate with each other and avoid being critical or judgemental. You endeavour to stay connected. Of course there will be ups and downs, and your relationship will inevitably go through periods of being distant or in conflict. And there will be plateau periods when not much is happening between you. But you will know how to reconnect and tap back into your closeness.

A thriving relationship enables you to exist in your own right and maintain your psychological integrity. The love, mutual support and acceptance that we give and receive in a loving relationship keeps it fresh and alive. And the affectionate and adoring feelings between you and your partner are sustained by your everyday activities with each other.

Remember to keep investing in your relationship by following these 10 principles.

1   Spend quality time with each other.

2   Be open and honest and don't withhold from each other.

3   Surprise each other with flowers, romantic dinners, notes, gifts, etc.

4   Plan time together and weekends away.

5   Stay curious about each other and commit to a feeling of adventure and aliveness in your relationship.

6   Cultivate your goodwill towards your partner.

7   Work on clarifying your boundaries.

8   Improve your communication skills.

9   Focus on the positive aspects of the relationship.

10   Become more self-disclosing and intimate.

If you feel good about each other and your relationship, you will do most if not all of these naturally. If, however, your relationship has lost its spark and you are taking each other for granted or feeling distant from each other, any of the above will help you to reconnect.

 **tip**

> Keep putting into practice everything you have learned about how to create a brilliant relationship and always remember that you deserve the very best.

See your relationship as a gift

Your relationship is a wonderful opportunity for you to deepen the richness of your life. The love between you and your partner will transform you and has the potential to heal the wounded part of you, if you surrender to it and commit to the journey together. Keep nurturing your relationship by focusing on what you love about your partner. Create balance in your own lifestyle by balancing your partner's needs with yours. Be spontaneous and playful. Tell your partner you love them, but don't just tell each other 'I love you'. Say what you *specifically* love about each other. Take the time to say something lovely that you've never said before. Give each other surprise gifts. Accept your partner for who they are. Laugh together. Be grateful for everything you have. And most of all enjoy each other and each moment.

Believe in your capacity to have a brilliant relationship and you will commit to making it happen.

Index